Chicken Soup for the Soul.

Simply Happy

D0012827

Chicken Soup for the Soul: Simply Happy
A Crash Course in Chicken Soup for the Soul Advice and Wisdom
Amy Newmark

Published by Chicken Soup for the Soul, LLC www.chickensoup.com
Copyright ©2016 by Chicken Soup for the Soul, LLC. and Amy Newmark.
All Rights Reserved.

The publisher gratefully acknowledges the many publishers and individuals
who granted Chicken Soup for the Soul permission to reprint the cited
material.

Photo of Amy Newmark courtesy of Susan Morrow at SwickPix
Cover and Interior by Daniel Zaccari

Distributed to the booktrade by Simon & Schuster. SAN: 200-2442

Publisher's Cataloging-In-Publication Data
(Prepared by The Donohue Group, Inc.)

Names: Newmark, Amy.
Title: Simply happy : a crash course in Chicken Soup for the Soul advice
    and wisdom / Amy Newmark.
Description: [Cos Cob, Connecticut] : Chicken Soup for the Soul, LLC
    [2016]
Identifiers: LCCN 2016949004 | ISBN 978-1-61159-949-7 (print) |
    ISBN 978-1-61159-254-2 (ebook)
Subjects: LCSH: Newmark, Amy. | Chicken soup for the soul. | Happiness. |
    Attitude (Psychology) | Conduct of life. | Self-help techniques.
Classification: LCC BF575.H27 N49 2016 (print) | LCC BF575.H27 (ebook) |
    DDC 158--dc23

PRINTED IN THE UNITED STATES OF AMERICA
on acid∞free paper

25 24 23 22 21 20 19 18 17 16   01 02 03 04 05 06 07 08 09 10 11

Simply Happy

A Crash Course in Chicken Soup for the Soul Advice and Wisdom

Amy Newmark

Chicken Soup for the Soul, LLC
Cos Cob, CT

Changing your life one story at a time®
www.chickensoup.com

Table of Contents

A Crash Course in Chicken Soup for the Soul Advice and Wisdom

My journey from Wall Street to Main Street

I was always a writer and storyteller but the tales that I told were about new products and management teams and corporate earnings. Useful? Yes. True? Yes. But as they say on Wall Street, the only two emotions in the stock market are fear and greed.

After years of analyzing stocks, running a hedge fund, doing investment banking, and serving on corporate boards, I was ready for a change. I wanted to tell stories that involved the whole range of human emotions, not just fear and greed! My husband Bill was looking for his next project, too, after running a large company with 5,000 employees.

Then we heard that Jack Canfield and Mark Victor Hansen were ready to hand their baby, Chicken Soup for the Soul, over to new owners, ones who would respect their legacy *and* take the company into the future.

This was going to be a *big* job, one filled with passion and purpose, but I was a brand-new empty nester, so why not?

Bill and I put on our business hats and analyzed the company's prospects, and we put on our philanthropic hats and imagined what we could do with this iconic brand to make the world a better place. If we were going to work this hard, there'd better be more to it than just making payroll!

While Bill was doing the legal and financial work, I was reading the old *Chicken Soup for the Soul* books — containing more than 10,000 stories — to understand what we were buying. That was *my* crash course in Chicken Soup for the Soul advice and wisdom, and it was life changing. I had never seen anything like this before, so much selfless sharing by people who were willing to pass on their best tips and their life experiences so that others could tweak or even completely reboot their own lives.

I was already a different person after reading those first 10,000+ personal, revealing stories, and now, nine years later, I've read tens of thousands more — the ones that we've published and the ones that were submitted by the public but not published.

Everyone tells me I've changed. I certainly feel different: more relaxed even though I'm working so hard; more compassionate and less judgmental; more grounded and grateful for everything that I have; and way more knowledgeable about what makes people tick. You can't read the intimate details of thousands of lives without growing and improving.

Now it's time for *your* crash course in Chicken Soup for the Soul advice and wisdom. I've distilled what I've learned from all those stories and from my own rather eclectic life experience into these pages — into simple, entertaining morsels.

I'm going to take you on the same journey that I've been on. I'll show you what I've learned and introduce you to the stories that have changed my life and the people who wrote them.

You'll read easy tips for recognizing the strengths that you *already* have, the *full toolkit* of skills and attributes that are already inside you. Our writers say they started out as ordinary people — and then they had some kind of extraordinary experience that revealed to them how much strength and talent and determination they had. We all have that good stuff inside us already and if you come away from these pages knowing only *that*, you will be a changed person. Once you realize that you already have your toolkit, you can be the mechanic for your own life.

This is a different kind of self-help book. It's based on the opinions of thousands of people, not one person. I've blended all that *wisdom* and all those *life experiences* into straightforward, simple pieces of advice that work. Most of these tips literally take *one second* to implement, because they involve a mere change in outlook. There are no seminars, no workbooks, and no programs to follow. It all happens in your head.

The chapters are short, the stories are fun to read, and there will be a lot of laughs along the way — because people are funny. I know you'll have a good time, and you'll come away re-energized and full of self-confidence and strategies for improving your everyday life and your future. You'll *feel good* about yourself.

And because I have that Wall Street view of life — practical and bottom line–oriented — you'll find that the tips in this book are realistic and do-able.

I don't like wasting my time or yours. That's why I've written this crash course for you — a quick, deep dive into the most essential tips for creating a happy, confident, positive life filled with passion and purpose.

Made a Difference to That One!

The original Chicken Soup for the Soul story that says it all

As my husband Bill and I prepared to take over Chicken Soup for the Soul nine years ago, I curled up on the comfy green couch in the family room over our garage and went on a book binge. Or, you might say, a *soup* binge.

What a huge responsibility I was taking on as the new publisher and editor-in-chief! For tens of millions of fans around the world, the books had become a portable support group of sorts — friends they could take off the bookshelf when they needed a laugh, a dose of positive thinking, or comfort during a tough time.

While Bill and his business partner handled the legal and financial details, my job was to understand the past and plan for the future. What had been published so far and what should we publish going forward? The company's founders, Jack Canfield and Mark Victor Hansen, had arranged for one of each book to be sent to us, and boxes and boxes of *Chicken Soup for the Soul* books had already arrived on our front doorstep.

So I put in my contact lenses early one morning, lined up those 150 or so books, sat on that green couch, and started feasting. I've always been a voracious reader — I was the little girl who would leave the children's room at the public library carrying a dozen books at a time, so this was a once-in-a-lifetime opportunity for me. I would sit and read every day for the next three months. Until then, I'd only read the original *Chicken Soup for the Soul* published in 1993 — the one that started it all. It was still on a bookshelf downstairs in our library.

Now, I devoured books for mothers and teenagers and dog lovers and gardeners. I laughed and cried along with fathers, veterans, nurses, and prisoners. I was inspired by tales for teachers, brides, cancer survivors, and Christian teens. The list went on and on, through more than 100 *Chicken Soup for the Soul* books on more than 100 different topics.

My head was spinning!

I was taking a risk doing all this reading on the green couch — the "magic couch," as my kids nicknamed it — because I had an inconvenient tendency to fall asleep on it as soon as I sat down. There was something about that couch! I was powerless to fight it. We often joked that I could have major surgery on the green couch without anesthesia because it had such an effect on me.

But I couldn't stop reading those *Chicken Soup for the Soul* books and I stayed awake. I even found that I had to change my contact lenses every week instead of every two weeks — because my tears of joy *and* sadness were clouding them.

I was astounded as I discovered that a book publisher was lurking inside me, after all those years on Wall Street and in the corporate world! I jotted down page after page of ideas for new book titles and new topics that would keep *Chicken Soup for the Soul* relevant and useful for our readers.

It was time to write the next chapter of my life.

***

Of the 10,000+ stories I read during my crash course, the one that affected me the most was from the original *Chicken Soup for the Soul*, the one that I took off my library bookshelf and re-read during my three-month Chicken Soup for the Soul immersion. It also happens to be one of the most popular stories in our library.

It's short, it's simple, and it summed up my mission. It might be one of those urban-legend stories that never actually happened, but I love it anyway because its message is real, universal, and timeless. Here it is in its entirety:

One at a Time

A friend of ours was walking down a deserted Mexican beach at sunset. As he walked along, he began to see another man in the distance. As he grew nearer, he noticed that the man kept leaning down, picking something up and throwing it out into the water. Time and again he kept hurling things out into the ocean.

As our friend approached even closer, he noticed that the man was picking up starfish that had been washed up on the beach and, one at a time, he was throwing them back into the water.

Our friend was puzzled. He approached the man and said, "Good evening, friend. I was wondering what you are doing."

"I'm throwing these starfish back into the ocean. You see, it's low tide right now and all of these starfish have been washed up onto the shore. If I don't throw them back into the sea, they'll die up here from lack of oxygen."

"I understand," my friend replied, "but there must be thousands of starfish on this beach. You can't possibly get to all of them. There are simply too many. And don't you realize this is probably happening on hundreds of beaches all up and down this coast? Can't you see that you can't possibly make a difference?"

The man smiled, bent down, and picked up yet another

starfish, and as he threw it back into the sea, he replied, "Made a difference to that one!"

The point of the story? Every little thing we do, no matter how small it may seem, *does* make a difference and is worth doing. Sometimes we forget this because our daily to-do lists seem overwhelming and the problems of the world insurmountable. We think we have no time to have an effect on the world or that it takes a big, dramatic gesture to have an impact. We wonder: *What can I possibly do to help when I barely have time to do my own laundry?*

The starfish story reminds us that it only takes a few seconds to change the world. If you pick up one piece of garbage from the sidewalk, it matters. If you catch one spider in a cup and take it outside instead of smashing it dead, it matters. If you let one driver merge in front of you in the mall parking garage exit line, it matters. And if you take one extra minute to do a small kindness for someone, it matters.

> *One small act can have a cascading, domino effect that first changes one person's day, then changes dozens of other people's days.*

That one small act can have a cascading, domino effect that first changes one person's day, then changes dozens of other people's days, and then maybe even changes the rest of someone's life in a profound way. Not that you'll ever know that your small act resulted in that big impact. And you probably aren't focused on that anyway. One of my favorite quotes is from a Canadian farmer named Nelson Henderson, who said, "The true meaning of life is to plant trees, under whose shade you do not expect to sit."

I'd venture to guess that simple starfish story has changed many lives, just as our more than 20,000 stories have. Little changes, big changes—they're all good. Change happens one story at a time. And that's our motto as we put together a new book every month in the bustling Chicken Soup for the Soul office in the friendly village of Cos Cob, Connecticut. We know that we are changing lives one story at a time and that every story we publish has the potential to make at least a small difference to hundreds of thousands of readers.

**

We get tons of fan mail from our readers — or maybe I should say we get screenfuls of fan *e-mails* from our readers — who tell us how a story or book has affected their lives. We read all the mail and we are grateful for the feedback. We work hard, so for us, too, every piece of fan mail makes a difference! There is one letter in particular that stands out. I think this story will "wow" you.

On the night of April 12, 2011 we got an e-mail from twenty-year-old, newly married, military wife Tracy Fitzgerald. She'd been a big fan of the *Chicken Soup for the Teenage Soul* books, so when she heard about *Chicken Soup for the Military Wife's Soul*, she rushed out to buy it.

Tracy's husband Griffin was in the Army and had been deployed to Afghanistan for a twelve-month tour one month earlier. The couple was expecting their first child, a girl, and Griffin had been due to get out of the Army that summer, just in time to see the birth of his daughter in July. Instead, he'd signed up for extended duty because he felt strongly about serving in Afghanistan.

Griffin had only been away for two weeks when Tracy started reading *Chicken Soup for the Military Wife's Soul*. She read a story every night... leading up to the night of April 11th.

That night, she read the story "Newfound Heroes" by Carol Howard.

"It's a story about a military wife like me who got a call from her husband while he was deployed because he had been shot and seriously injured," Tracy explained in her e-mail. "While reading the story I kept stopping to think about how I would react if I received a similar phone call. When I read that, despite his injuries, her husband could still walk, I wondered what we would do if my husband called to say he had lost his legs. I thought about how we would manage, how difficult it would be, and how our lives would change."

Then, a new thought came to her mind.

"I imagined the two of us with our little girl, only she was about five and playing at the beach. My husband and I were holding hands and smiling. Everything was okay and it didn't seem so different after all. I told myself that no matter what… things would be okay."

After Tracy finished reading the story, she fell asleep — only to be jolted awake the next morning by a phone call from her husband. She hadn't heard from him for a week, so she was relieved to hear his voice… until he fell silent, and then announced, "I'm coming home." Tracy was overjoyed but confused. Was the Army sending troops home already?

> "The true meaning of life is to plant trees, under whose shade you do not expect to sit."

"Why?" she asked.

"I've been hit by an IED," he said. The bomb had blown off Griffin's right leg from the knee down, his ring finger on his right hand, the tip of his right pinkie, and had caused multiple shrapnel wounds on his left thigh and both hands.

At first Tracy cried, but then she tried to be strong for her husband as they finished their brief phone call. "I tried to hold it together as much as I could for him," she wrote. "It wasn't until after we got off the phone that I let myself cry until I couldn't any longer."

As the sad day wore on, Tracy felt herself growing stronger, with a new perspective on the tragedy. She said, "I realized everything happens for a reason, and as unfortunate as this is, my husband still has his life. He's going to witness his child being born and he won't have to worry about missing a thing."

Tracy wrote, "Reading that story in *Chicken Soup for the Military Wife's Soul* gave me the foresight I needed. It gave me the strength to see the big picture. It prepared me for what was to come without knowing it. You never know your strength until being strong is the only option. And you could never guess how you will act in a certain situation; you can only prepare for it. I don't know how I would have reacted had I not read 'Newfound Heroes' and thought about being in a similar situation, the night before my husband's call. It might have been more difficult for me to see the big picture."

Tracy's e-mail made the rounds in our office and had quite an impact. One story in one book had made a significant difference to one of our readers. We were sad for her and Griffin, and even more aware of the importance of that time we spend glued to our computers choosing the stories that go into our books.

It's like the starfish story that I love so much. We can't help everyone out there, but we sure can help a lot of them — one person at a time, one story at a time. In Tracy Fitzgerald's case, we "made a difference to that one." And I'm happy to report that Tracy and Griffin are doing great. Here they are with their five-year-old daughter and their two-year-old son in a wonderful photo, courtesy of Amber Phinisee Photography.

CHAPTER

—2—

A Smile Is a Boomerang

They're free, they're easy, and they change your whole day

One of my favorite jokes—probably because it's short enough for me to remember—is the one I heard from a tour guide while on a family vacation in Australia. After doing the Sydney Bridge climb, getting up close and personal with kangaroos on a golf course, and visiting the famous Uluru red rock in the Northern Territory, Bill and I took our four kids to a tropical rainforest in the northeast corner of Queensland. There, after an unfortunately intimate experience with dozens of leeches, we got to witness an iconic Australian pastime when our khaki-clad tour guide took a boomerang from his bag.

"What do Australians call a boomerang that doesn't come back, mate?" he asked, as he lobbed it through the air.

I shook my head, watching as the boomerang spun in the air, turned around, and flew right back into his hand.

"A stick!" he laughed, slapping his knee.

That was fifteen years ago and I'm still telling that joke, even though my kids call me a dork when I do. The boomerang, credited to Australia's indigenous people, was a great invention. If you threw one and you failed to hit your target the boomerang would come right back to you and nothing was lost.

Smiles are like boomerangs. When you throw them out there, they invariably come right back at you—unless you're an American tourist in Australia trying to throw a boomerang for the first time while your four tired and sullen teenagers watch you.

If you encounter someone grouchy, throw out that smile boomerang and see what happens. My experience is that people will usually smile back at you. You might even have a better day because your smile will change the way people react to you. And in the few cases where your smile isn't returned, nothing is lost.

We've published many stories that illustrate the power of smiling, including one of my favorites, by Cristy Trandahl, called "Let's Face It," in *Chicken Soup for the Soul: My Resolution.*

> *"A smile is the light in your window that tells others that there is a caring, sharing person inside."*

Cristy says that she walked into her local convenience store one day, in a hurry, with half a dozen kids waiting outside in the van, and she heard the cashier whisper to her co-worker, "What a crabby-looking lady."

She was intrigued and looked for the "crabby lady" as she hurried through the aisles, grabbing things and throwing them in her basket. Finally, she caught sight of the lady. "Crabby wasn't the word," Cristy said. "This lady looked like she had smelled something really bad."

It took a moment before, in shock, Cristy realized something — she was looking into the store's security mirror… at her own reflection! *She* was the crabby-looking lady!

That night, after she got the kids to bed, Cristy threw herself on her own bed and sobbed. She had been voted "the girl with the nicest smile" in her high school class. What had happened to her?

Cristy made a simple resolution: to smile. She didn't wait for January first; she started right then. It took practice, but over time smiling became more natural for her. She started by making a conscious effort to smile at least ten times a day — and it couldn't be ten times in a row. She had to spread the smiles out over the day. After a month, Cristy found that smiling was becoming easier, even when something was happening that would have caused a frown in the past.

Her hallelujah moment came nine months later when she rushed into a coffee shop to meet some friends, running behind as usual. Cristy overheard the cashier remark to a co-worker, "There's that happy-looking lady again."

* * *

I think I first realized the power of smiling when my friend Michelle — a stockbroker and crusader against fraudulent companies on Wall Street — was sent to federal prison for a securities industry violation in 2003.

Even though she'd been unfairly convicted (for an illegal act committed by one of her clients) she was sentenced to four years. By the time she arrived at Danbury Federal Prison Camp, many of her so-called friends and clients had abandoned her.

I felt awful for her and although she was more of a business friend than a social one, I decided I would visit her at least once a month during her incarceration. Her kids would see her on weekends and I would provide some relief during the week. She was not too far from me, about an hour's drive, but with my busy work schedule and two teenagers at home, I knew it would be a bit difficult. I was committed, but I wondered if I'd be able to stick to my plan.

I remember vividly the first time I saw Michelle walk through the locked doors of the holding area into the visiting room. I didn't know what to expect because I knew she was miserable; after all, she was a single mother who was constantly worried about how her teenage kids were doing without her. I figured she'd come out depressed, scared, or in tears.

Nope. The doors opened and Michelle emerged in her khaki prisoner uniform, striding past the guards and into the visiting room with a big, broad smile across her face. And she did that every time, even when the guards held her outside the door for what seemed like forever, for no good reason, cutting into our visiting time.

Michelle's smile made me feel *great.*

Her smile felt like a reward, as if my being there really mattered. I'm guessing part of her smiling was that she was happy to have a visitor. But also, I knew she must have been making the Herculean effort to put on that smile for my benefit, and that was brilliant of her. She must have known the effect a smile has on people no matter where you are or what the situation, because it worked on me — it motivated me to keep going to see her. We all respond better to someone who is smiling and upbeat — you *want* to be with that person. Even the guards seemed to like her.

Her smile made me feel so good that I found a way to go back each month. I was such a regular that I started recognizing the other ladies and *their* visitors. I even nodded *hello* to Piper Kerman of *Orange Is the New Black* fame — she was one of the Camp residents at that time too, and my friend was one of the minor characters in her book.

Even when Michelle was moved from the Camp to the regular prison at Danbury for the nine-month substance abuse program that many of the white-collar criminals signed up for (it took nine months off your total sentence if you did it), I still kept going each month. That was not a fun place to visit. Unlike the Camp, which was relatively relaxed, at the big prison there were murderers, and I had to go through a scary locking-door system to get into the visiting room. One time I got stuck there for an extra hour during a lockdown or headcount or something, and — here comes the suburban mom part — I was quite anxious to get out of there because I was going to be late to my daughter's soccer game and I was the team mother.

I visited Michelle faithfully for two and a half years until she was moved to a halfway house to finish her sentence. I'd like to think I would have done it anyway, but it sure was easier because of that broad smile of hers and how it made me feel.

The renowned motivational speaker and author Denis Waitley said, "A smile is the light in your window that tells others that there is a caring, sharing person inside."

That's what my friend's smile did. Ironically, I thought it would be *my* smile that would keep *her* going during our monthly visits but it ended up being *her* smile that kept *me* going.

* * *

My friend Sophfronia Scott, a talented novelist and writing coach, is always smiling. She says she was inspired by a story written by Hanoch McCarty in the original *Chicken Soup for the Soul* book. She wrote about her reaction in her story "Living by the Light of a Smile" in *Chicken Soup for the Soul: Reader's Choice*.

> *Your smile will change the way people react to you.*

The story that changed everything for Sophfronia was about the famous French writer Antoine de Saint-Exupéry, who wrote *The Little Prince* as well as a lesser-known piece, "The Smile," which was possibly based on his own experience as a captured fighter pilot in the Spanish Civil War. He describes a pilot, facing execution the next day, who makes a connection with his jailer when their eyes lock unexpectedly. The pilot smiles at his jailer and the two men begin to discuss their families and even share pictures. Later, after the jailer allows the pilot to escape, he reports, "My life was saved by a smile."

That story had a big impact on Sophfronia. The morning after she read it, she stopped in a deli and ordered a cup of tea, smiling and saying "thank you" when the server handed her the cup. He looked confused at first, but then he smiled back and said, "I've been doing this all morning and you're the first person to smile at me."

Sophfronia was a new college graduate who had recently moved to New York City. She had believed that smiling was not a good idea in the "big, bad city" because it would attract unwanted attention, so she'd been maintaining a neutral expression on her face and avoiding connections with strangers.

But after she read about Saint-Exupéry and she smiled at the man in the deli, Sophfronia says, "I couldn't believe how good I felt—I actually felt more like myself! As I continued to smile throughout the days, weeks and months I noticed an amazing cycle: The more I smiled, the friendlier everything seemed; and the friendlier everything seemed, the more I smiled. It also seemed to me that the smiles I received in return were not just polite smiles. I felt a momentary connection with the person, as though we had come to an agreement that all was right with the world."

She realized that smiles were not a sign of weakness. No! Smiling gave her strength. She could change the people she met just by smiling at them. She shares a wonderful quote from Andy Andrews' book, *The Traveler's Gift*: "My smile has become my calling card. It is, after all, the most potent weapon I possess."

Sophfronia says that while boxers may lead with their left or right jabs, she leads with her smile, the one that lights up the world for her. She closes her story by saying, "My life is so much brighter, so much more joyous, that I can't imagine how I lived without such light."

***

So that's it. Our second shared lesson—about using the power of smiling to create all those smile boomerangs that will come right back at you. It works.

Imagine what could happen: You smile at someone at eight

in the morning, and that person smiles at someone else as a result, and that someone else smiles at two more people, and by eight o'clock that night, who knows?

Maybe your 8 a.m. smile turned into 100 smiles that wouldn't have otherwise occurred that day.

Maybe it even changed a life.

CHAPTER
— 3 —

Meet Your
Biggest Critic

That little voice in your head is your
worst enemy

Remembering to smile is relatively easy. That's a tip you can implement quickly. I'm going to share some more "quick and easy" tips and changes in this book, and also some that take a little more time and effort to incorporate into your life.

In this chapter, I want to share a big, important change that you probably need to make if you're one of those perfectionist, type A, striving-for-excellence types like me. This change will take a little more work, but it's basically an "umbrella" change — something that needs to overlay whatever else you're doing.

Here it is: *Go easier on yourself* — be less of a perfectionist, less judgmental about your own weaknesses. And most importantly, don't be so critical of your performance. Stop listening to that negative little voice inside your own head.

There's something that psychologists call "Impostor Syndrome" and it's pretty common in busy, successful people, especially women. It happens when you start wondering when the rest of the world will realize that you don't know what you're doing. You may be doing something beautifully, as well as anyone on the planet could do it, but you still feel like you're pretending — that you're not qualified to do this magnificent thing that you're already doing!

I often feel like this — even now, after all these years doing fairly cool things — especially when I'm attempting something new. I was filled with self-doubt when faced with hosting our PBS television special, or appearing on a national morning television show without knowing what they were going to ask me, or even writing this memoir/self-help book, which is different from the previous 132 books that I've edited and written, because those books include 101 stories by other people.

I already delayed this book for a year — it was originally scheduled for October 2015. Luckily, I have an understanding publisher — *moi* — so I put it off until I had the confidence to do it. Which I appear to have now!

I think that even after creating all those *Chicken Soup for the Soul* books and writing a nationally syndicated weekly newspaper column for years, I still felt a little insecure about presuming to tell *you* things. That little voice in my head was still making me think, *Who am I to tell people how to improve their lives?*

> Stop listening to that negative little voice inside your own head.

Here's what finally convinced me to sit down and write this book: my new podcast. We launched the Chicken Soup for the Soul podcast in February 2016 and we've been pleased with its performance. The daily download numbers are excellent — and I'm getting fan mail and all kinds of positive reinforcement. I feel a little like Sally Field when she accepted her Oscar in 1985 and famously told the crowd, "You *like* me!"

I was asked to do the podcast only weeks before I started it, and I had never even listened to one before. I didn't even know there was a Podcasts icon on my iPhone. But I dreamed up a whole series, wrote the scripts, went off to the recording studio, and started performing them. And it *is* a performance. This from the girl who was always stuck with being the narrator in the school plays instead of getting a more fun, more prestigious acting role (because "you're so good at memorizing things, dear").

By doing the podcast I found my voice! I finally realized that the combination of my life experience and all these awesome Chicken Soup for the Soul stories translates into interesting, digestible tidbits of advice, and that I know how to share them effectively with you. After doing the podcast for a couple of months, I was able to sit down and start writing. Now I view this book as another way to share my favorite stories and my best advice with you, just as I do on the podcast.

I've continued having bouts of self-doubt while writing this book — who wouldn't? You'd have to be an egomaniac to breeze through writing your first real book — part memoir, no less — without some insecurity.

At least I know I'm in good company. So many successful people confess to being insecure — to having Impostor Syndrome. I bet it happens to you too — when doing your normal awesome things or when you try something new. It can even happen when you are doing a routine thing, such as watching your kids. I experienced Impostor Syndrome hard, like a whack in the face, doing just that, about twenty-five years ago, and I still remember it vividly.

My first husband, Phil, and I had gone to our neighbors' house for a barbecue with our two young children, who were still toddlers. Phil had to leave halfway through the afternoon to embark on a business trip, so I stayed on with the kids. As I was walking Mike and Ella to the car after the party ended, they looked up at me expectantly with those trusting little faces, confident they were in good hands. I was suddenly hit with a massive wave of insecurity.

Here's what a little voice in my head was telling me: "You're not really a grownup. You're barely out of college." But I had these two little people depending on me — two of *them* and only one *me*. They thought I knew what I was doing. That little voice continued: "How can *you* possibly take care of *them*?"

I did my best to ignore my inner critic and I drove us home, got the kids out of their car seats and into the house, and then made my way through dinner and baths and bedtime. I pretended that I was their all-knowing, competent mother instead of the kid I felt like. It worked and the *actual* kids were none the wiser.

We get some revealing stories about this negative voice in our heads from our writers. In a story titled "Battling My Inner Bully" in *Chicken Soup for the Soul: The Power of Positive*, Sara Matson describes how, even in grade school, her inner bully was much worse than any bully she encountered in class. Sara says that a boy named Scott used to call her Fat Lips every chance he got. He'd sit behind her on the school bus, teasing her, kicking her seat, or flicking her head with a pencil.

Of course, now that I'm an adult and watched the same kind of thing happen to my daughter, I know what that was probably about. That boy Scott actually thought Sara was cute, and he did that dumb thing that boys do to get attention from a girl they like. Nonetheless, it was bullying and it made Sara miserable. She still reflects on it, but she says that her own negative inner voice was much worse than anything Scott ever did to her back in her school days.

Sara says, "I grew up lacking self-confidence, even though outwardly I was a high achiever. I excelled in school, earned a full scholarship to college, graduated *magna cum laude*, and became a world-traveling teacher. But I couldn't fully enjoy those accomplishments, because always, underneath, was the feeling that I wasn't good enough."

Eventually, as an adult, Sara went to a therapist to figure out why she couldn't quiet that negative inner voice. She still didn't manage to overcome it—until she was diagnosed with an autoimmune disease called Sjögren's syndrome.

"The diagnosis explained years of aches and pains, a troubled pregnancy, and the loss of my sense of smell," says Sara. Her chiropractor recommended that she try therapy again, pointing out that "how people think greatly affects their physical health."

This time, Sara found a cozy, wise, spiritual woman named Vicki. And Sara had a breakthrough. She was explaining Sjögren's syndrome to Vicki and said, "It's an autoimmune disease. My white blood cells attack my own moisture-producing glands." Suddenly it struck Sara: "That's funny," she said. "I just realized, that's what I do. I attack my own self."

That insight changed Sara. On her fortieth birthday, she wrote in her journal: "This year, I want to be kind to myself." She says it has been hard work, but she has learned to talk back to that little voice in her head, saying things like "I didn't do that perfectly, but it was good enough," or "Everyone says things they wish they hadn't," or "Good people are human and make mistakes."

I had an epiphany of my own while writing this chapter and talking to my friend Natasha Stoynoff, a Chicken Soup for the Soul coauthor who gave me great advice and feedback on this book. I have an autoimmune disease too — Grave's eye disease. I got the

> *"It's hard to fight an enemy who has outposts in your head."*

diagnosis while writing this book, after more than two decades of wondering why my eyelids were so wide open, showing the whites of my eyes above my blue irises. The ophthalmologist told me that stress can bring on autoimmune diseases. When I look at old photos, I see that my eyelids started popping open wider and wider during the exact same period that I described above — the time when I had two toddlers and I started doubting myself, just like Sara Matson. My marriage to my high school sweetheart was falling apart during that time, too, so there was an awful lot of negativity in my life. I was very down on myself.

By the time I got divorced, when the kids were ages seven and nine, the eye problem had gotten worse and I was all googly-eyed. Even though it was a civilized divorce — we didn't use lawyers and we still get along well today — divorce and everything leading up to it can be very stressful. I wonder if my self-doubt and stress helped to bring on that autoimmune disease.

I remarried in 1999, adding two wonderful stepchildren to my life as well as my new husband, Bill. Bill is a great influence — supportive, always complimenting me — and he has truly brought out the best in me and helped me mute that negative voice in my head so that it only pipes up occasionally now, when I am doing something new.

The damage to my eyelids was permanent so I just had surgery to try to make them look normal again. As I'm making one more pass through this manuscript in early July, I am sitting home with two black eyes and a couple of very swollen eyelids. I hope to have normal eyelids by the time I do the publicity tour for this book in three months!

There's a quote that I love from the author Sally Kempton. She says, "It's hard to fight an enemy who has outposts in your head." Absolutely. And that's the point of this chapter. Before we conquer the world, we have to conquer our *own* negative little voices. I'm still working on it myself!

CHAPTER
—4—

Life Is a Happy Mess
Strive for excellence, not perfection

Now that you've quelled that negative little voice in your head — your built-in critic — let's talk about your perfectionism. I know it's there, because you're interested enough in improving *something* about your life that you're reading this book! But this book isn't about perfecting anything; it's about having a happy life, and that means accepting *less than perfection*.

Unless you are working for NASA and building a million-dollar door handle for a spaceship, *it doesn't have to be perfect.* This is something I've learned over many years of 1) being a busy mom with not enough time, 2) being a human being, and 3) sending 132 books to the printer, every single one with invisible typos that do not show up until we've printed at least 50,000 copies.

I've learned that muddling through life accepting that I will always operate at somewhere between 90 and 95% is about as good as it gets. If I can do three things well (but not perfectly) at any given time — and 90% is still pretty awesome — that's a total score of 270 points of "getting stuff done" — versus spending hours or days obsessing over one thing and getting it 99% perfect but dropping the ball in a major way on the other two. I get 270 points my way, versus 99 points the striving-for-perfection way.

Like most people, I have juggled many different full-time roles in my life — the main three being mother, wife, and executive. There were never enough hours in the day to fulfill each role as completely as I wanted when I was raising my kids.

There were nights when the kids needed me to stay home and help with homework but I had to attend a business dinner with Bill because he needed me more that particular night. There were other nights when Bill got the short end of the stick, because I needed to put the kids first. And if I somehow managed to do all the kid stuff *and* husband stuff, then the work stuff would suffer.

When I was an equity analyst on Wall Street, one of my analyst friends would spend hours and hours perfecting his earnings spreadsheets — the ones where he would try to predict a company's future earnings so that investors could decide whether or not to buy that company's stock. They were only estimates anyway, guaranteed to be wrong, but my friend wouldn't listen when I suggested to him that he leave well enough alone and get a life.

> *"Striving for excellence motivates you; striving for perfection is demoralizing."*

A wonderful psychologist and expert on stress management named Harriet Braiker wrote the breakthrough book, *The Type E Woman: How to Overcome the Stress of Being Everything to Everybody*. Harriet said: "Striving for excellence motivates you; striving for perfection is demoralizing."

Women in particular, with all their multitasking, need some help in letting go. Does anyone actually remember if you baked everything yourself the last time you entertained, if your kids' clothes looked perfectly pressed during the five minutes before they got mud on them, or if you sent out holiday cards every year without fail?

One of my favorite stories on this topic is "The Power of Illusion," in which Donna Milligan Meadows tells us about her friend Sara, who had the perfect home, with a beautifully wallpapered living room. One day, Donna was admiring Sara's house and lamenting that her own wallpaper didn't line up at the seams and wasn't straight at the ceiling.

"It's all an illusion," Sara told her. "The details don't matter. Look at my seams; they aren't perfect either. There is a tear over in the corner. You did your wallpaper yourself so you know every spot that isn't exactly right. No one else will see the mistakes, just like you didn't see mine."

Years later, Donna was days away from hosting her daughter's wedding in her perfectly landscaped back yard, where the flowers even matched the wedding color scheme. Then the rains came. The grass developed a fungus and mushrooms sprouted everywhere. Donna was panic-stricken until she remembered Sara's gentle voice saying: "It's all an illusion. The details don't matter."

The wedding ended up being perfect, or at least the "perfect illusion of a fairy tale wedding in a magical place." Donna strove for excellence, and while she didn't achieve 100% perfection, she got close and I'm sure that her daughter and their guests would say to this day that it *was* the perfect wedding.

That story came from *Chicken Soup for the Soul: Think Positive*, the biggest selling book that we have published under my "regime" and one that is a constant source of inspiration for me. The 101 stories in that book cover everything from hugely important life episodes like death and illness, to the everyday ups and downs of life — stuff like getting a stain on your carpet.

You can probably recite the history of certain stains on your carpet — when they happened, who was to blame, and you can walk right over to them and point them out. So here's a way to stop caring about them: turn them into souvenirs of a life well lived. Let me tell you another great story from our *Think Positive* book — Nikki Deckon's "Magic Stains."

The myriad stains on her carpets embarrassed Nikki. She says when someone new came over, she wanted to shout, "I'm really not this gross! Just don't look down! Ignore the nasty carpet!"

That's no way to live, right? You don't want to be embarrassed and apologizing all the time for your home. After all, you live there. It's your haven and the place where you and your family are… a family!

One day, one of Nikki's friends told her to stop apologizing for the well-worn state of her house. She suggested that instead Nikki should be grateful to her home. She should start thanking all her possessions for being part of her life, for *being there* for her family.

She told Nikki about a group of people who conducted an experiment. After they'd used an item, like a rake, they'd thank it for its kind service and gently put it away. Eventually, this community of people discovered that they were quite successful and highly productive. They attributed it to thanking their daily tools out loud.

Nikki decided to try it. She felt weird talking to a bunch of inanimate objects, so she decided to thank God instead. She thanked God for her family's furniture and the roof they slept under and their comfy pillows and clean towels (at least when she had time to do the laundry).

> Enjoy the happy mess of your busy, not quite perfect life.

Then Nikki got to her dining room carpet. She tried to find something nice to say about it, starting with the big, orange stain beneath her three-year-old's chair.

And she realized something. She and her three-year-old had made that stain while doing a fun art project. As Nikki looked around the living room and dining room she recalled each event that had caused a stain on the carpet: hours of play dough, a family pizza night, a coffee spill when her boys wrestled with her, and so on.

Nikki said, "I realized that all the stains represented something far lovelier than a clean carpet. They pointed to the fact that we were living our lives, with laughter and tears and messy projects and yummy dinners. We were alive! In our home we don't forbid laughter or the messes that often come with everyday life. Our home isn't sterile or oppressed. It is magical."

The British poet John Dryden said, "If you have lived, take thankfully the past." And that's how I view the wear and tear and the stains and the scratches and all those other little scars in my house — as souvenirs of good times.

The red salsa stain on the beige carpet happened the year we had almost thirty people for Christmas Eve and some people had to sit on cushions around a low coffee table. The sticky sap on the living room ceiling has been there ever since I bought a Christmas tree that was too tall and it scraped the ceiling. Now I use that spot as the marker for where the tree should go. The stains on my dining room carpet are from various friends and family members, some who are *guaranteed* to drop something *every* time they are here. We gladly take their stains so that we can spend time with them.

I've learned to make friends with those stains, dings, and bruises in my home and on my furniture. They show that we are actually *living* here.

***

So far, this chapter has been about things you can see — clean or dirty homes, perfect wedding venues, books surgically cleansed of every single typo — but what about the other ways that we Type A people try to be perfect? Parenting, for example. Every parent feels some guilt at times. You can't be there every moment and you want so badly to be the best mom or dad ever. But as I said earlier, life is about compromise and you have to work, and volunteer, and care for elderly parents, and take a long walk by yourself once in a while, even though you may feel you should be on duty 100% of the time for the kids.

I wrote about this in a book that I made as a gift for all the moms coming up behind me: *Chicken Soup for the Soul: The Multitasking*

Mom's Survival Guide. This book contains many of my personal stories, including this one that I titled "Coasting."

I was blessed with a career as a financial analyst while I was raising my kids. I could work from home and I could also ratchet up or down my commitment depending on how much time I had available to work. I was even able to take a whole year off when I moved from New York City to the suburbs and had my second child. Then I gradually ramped up the job again, ultimately doing it full-time from home.

With the proliferation of cell phones things got even easier. I remember talking to one of my traders while watching a bunch of kids on the roller coaster at a local amusement park one day and thinking *I can't believe I am trading stocks and chaperoning a class trip at the same time*. I even ran my own hedge fund from home — after all, the market was only open from 9:30-4:00 — so I could trade during the day, spend the afternoon and evening with the kids, and then prepare for the next trading day after they went to bed.

My kids were two years apart, so I had twenty years of childrearing until the second one turned eighteen and went off to college. I managed to work from home for seventeen and a half of those twenty years. The problem was the other two and a half years, when my kids were preteens, during which I commuted to New York City and traveled all over the country in a very intense senior executive position with a technology start-up. I also got divorced and moved twice during that same period.

Those years were my undoing as a multitasking mom, or so I thought. I had managed to be class mom every single year, alternating between the two kids, and I did lunch duty, drove on numerous field trips, and did other volunteer work for school and sports. But during those couple of bad years, I felt completely disconnected from school, not really knowing what was going on, not signing up for volunteer work, and not driving on a single field trip.

I wasn't even home for the emergency phone calls. My son was a "frequent flier" at the local emergency room and I would get calls at work, an hour away from home, with scary messages like "there isn't enough skin left to put in the stitches" and "he was only not breathing while he was unconscious." The worst was when I got a call that Mike rode his bike, unauthorized, of course, down an icy, rocky trail through the woods and was found lying in the dirt at the end of a dead-end road. He ended up in an ambulance and I almost quit my job that day.

But the New York City job ended and things went back to normal. I was once again class mom, team mom, driver, and volunteer, juggling my work-at-home career and all the mom duties I could handle. I still felt guilty about those two and a half lost years, however. That is, until I discussed those years with my kids, and they both told me exactly which field trips I drove on. They vividly remembered me participating in all my motherly duties during those commuting years, and yet I checked my calendar and I really hadn't! There is a great piece of poetry from T.S. Eliot that includes the following lines:

Footfalls echo in the memory
Down the passage which we did not take
Towards the door we never opened

That poem describes exactly what happened in my family. My kids gave me credit during my commuting years for driving on field trips, being class mom, and all the other wonderful things that I had stopped doing, but which I had done in earlier years. Somehow, I got a pass and was able to "coast" through those two and a half years, living off my good reputation. The kids are absolutely certain, to this day, that I never took a break from being the fabulous multitasking mom that I most certainly was not during that time. It just shows, your kids won't be nearly as critical of you as you will be of yourself. You have a little leeway. I only wish I had known that at the time.

And that's the point. Don't beat yourself up. Your quest for excellence, which *can't* and *shouldn't* produce perfection, is fine. You look like a superstar to everyone else, because you *are* a superstar. Enjoy the happy mess of your busy, not quite perfect life, and remember that everyone else thinks you are amazing and wishes *they* could be as good as you *already* are.

CHAPTER

— 5 —

Make Friends
with Your Body

Love it, nurture it, use it

Okay then. You've stopped listening to your inner critic (Chapter 3) and you've abandoned your quest for perfection (Chapter 4). You have one more task to complete before we move on in this crash course of Chicken Soup for the Soul wisdom! It's time to make friends with your body.

Your body is as much *you* as your brain is *you*. It's *all* you. And you can't really implement any of the tips and advice in this book if you're not friends with yourself. Stop thinking about your body as a separate entity that sometimes needs refurbishment, renovation, or repair, or that doesn't meet with your approval. Your body is as much you as your parents are you and your children are you. You wouldn't give them back, right? So embrace your unique body and get to know it.

I'm coauthoring a book with the world's first full-figured supermodel, Emme, who you may remember from when she burst onto the scene in the 1990s. Emme is a beautiful, healthy, athletic woman who exuberantly experiences life. Even though she had a stepfather who would point out to her where he thought she should lose weight — making her stand in her underwear as he drew big, black circles around the offending areas on her thighs and stomach with a thick magic marker — Emme didn't let him undermine her confidence. At Syracuse University, she rowed crew on a full athletic scholarship, and upon graduation she became a reporter and news anchor before joining the modeling world. Emme is the go-to person these days for the media when they want to talk about body image — the new "curvy" conversation. She was the person they interviewed when Mattel came out with Curvy Barbie in early 2016 and when *Sports Illustrated* put out their annual swimsuit issue featuring a plus-size model and female athletes, including on the front cover.

I was first introduced to Emme by our mutual friend, Natasha Stoynoff, who said I had to meet this dynamic champion for self-esteem and fitness, and that I should seriously consider making a book with her. So on the last day of January, a Sunday, my husband drove me down to the diner across from the YMCA in our town, where I was to meet the famous Emme. Ironically, I was having the worst flare-up of my bad back in years, so I was barely able to get in and out of the car, which was why Bill had to drive me. I crept up the diner's front steps, hunched over and pulling myself up by gripping the railing. And there was Emme waiting for me in a booth, sitting tall and strong in her workout clothes, with her wet, blond hair pulled straight back from her face that was flushed from swimming laps at the Y. Boy did I feel weak and small and seriously *un*athletic next to her.

> *Your body is as much you as your brain is you.*

Emme and I talked about one of her key messages — that you should *love* your body, *nurture* your body, and *use* your body. I borrowed the subtitle for this chapter from her. She talked about how you need to integrate your mind and your body and view yourself as one whole being, not a person who has a brain and then has this appendage — a body.

The book we are coauthoring — *Chicken Soup for the Soul: Curvy & Confident* — comes out at the end of 2016, for what retailers call the "New Year New You" season in January and February 2017. It has a beautiful cover shot of Emme by New York City–based photographer Shinsuke Kishima and it will be a different kind of New Year's resolution book! It will be all about Emme's message — about integrating what you view as *yourself* with your body. One way to do that is to feed your body, not deprive it of the nutrition it needs. And my favorite way to integrate my body into my whole self is to *use* it. In my case, that usually means going for a brisk three-mile walk in my hilly neigborhood.

The key is to move your body, work up a little sweat, and breathe a little faster. You'll feel energized and invigorated afterwards, and virtuous and proud of yourself, too. If you like to walk, then walk. If you like to dance in your underwear when nobody's looking, do that. Do you like to go rock climbing? Do that. Do whatever makes you happy and makes you move, whether it's kickboxing or aerobics, or something a little bit embarrassing, like doing deep knee bends every time your dog stops to sniff something while you are walking him.

What *not* to do? Don't do an exercise just because some expert on TV does it. You have to do what you like or you won't stick to it.

That was one of the messages from Richard Simmons, who wrote the foreword and the first story for our 2011 New Year New You book, *Chicken Soup for the Soul: Shaping the New You.* I asked Richard to work with us because he has the same down-to-earth message as Emme: eat what you like, in moderation, and exercise any way you like, as long as you have fun. And love the body you were issued at birth!

Richard, by the way, was a pleasure to work with. You might think that guy in shorts cracking jokes and flirting with the ladies isn't a serious businessman. But he was incredibly professional, on time, and friendly. And by the way, he's an excellent writer, too!

Richard invited our editorial team to his Slimmons exercise studio in LA to see him in action. So one time when I was out in LA on business, our Associate Publisher D'ette Corona, Senior Editor

Barbara LoMonaco, and I put on our exercise clothes and went to class. It was so much fun, and packed with fit, gorgeous men and women. They all looked like those perfect Hollywood people that we Connecticut suburbanites feel somewhat cowed by. The three of us had been practicing our aerobics at home for a couple of months before we went there, but that intense class was still quite a challenge. Here we are, still able to stand, *before* the class started: me, Richard, Barbara, and D'ette.

One of the stories that Richard highlighted in his foreword to the book was one of my favorites too. When a story stays in my head for years you know it's a powerful one. And this one is powerful, but simple too. It's by Douglas Brown, and it's called "What Did I Have to Lose?" Doug's inspirational tale started with his shirts — they were too tight and the buttons kept popping open. He also wasn't thrilled that he was buying pants with a fifty-inch waist.

But what really got to Doug was what happened when he applied for life insurance. His employer had offered to pay for $250,000 of life insurance for all the employees, but they had to qualify. Doug got his medical records together and spent over $40 on copying fees. Three weeks later he got a letter from the insurance provider saying, "We have decided not to offer you life insurance."

Doug was forty-six years old and very unfit. He needed to make a change but he didn't know where to start. He wanted to exercise but he also knew himself — if he joined a gym, he would stop going after a few weeks. He needed something that he could do every day without having to go out of his way to do it.

So Doug decided he would start taking the stairs in his office building, all the way up to his fourth-floor office.

He says the hardest thing was taking that first step. The first morning, the three flights of stairs looked like Mount Everest to him. But he told himself that even climbing Mount Everest required taking one step after another. One step at a time, sweating and wheezing, he made it to his office.

Our hero kept climbing the stairs in his building, going up and down as necessary, and soon he was up to twenty flights of stairs per day. He was feeling better but he needed to do more. So he added a one-mile walk during his break.

Then he got a letter from his employer's insurance company stating that they would reimburse him for part of the cost of a weight loss program. There was even a program that would meet in his office building every week. Doug learned about mindful eating in the program — actually thinking about what he was eating, not just stuffing his face.

After nine months of climbing the stairs, walking during the day, and thinking more about what he was eating, Doug lost eighty-five pounds and fourteen inches off his waistline. Now he's shocked when he looks at his old pictures.

What I love about this story, and what I have retained from it all these years, is that simple advice: take the stairs. The Chicken Soup for the Soul office is three floors up from the basement garage in our building. Now, unless I'm carrying a lot of heavy stuff, I take the stairs to and from the office. It's not much but it's something. And every morning when I get to work and consider pushing that elevator button, I think about Doug's story. And then I take the stairs.

I put a great quote at the beginning of that story when we published it. It's by Joan Welsh and here's how it goes: "A man's health can be judged by which he takes two at a time—pills or stairs."

Doug's story was the first one in *Chicken Soup for the Soul: Shaping the New You* after Richard Simmons' story, a place of honor in our books. We also make sure that we end our books with something very special and in that book, Story 101, our closer, was "Three Easy Steps" by Linda Rivers.

> "A man's health can be judged by which he takes two at a time— pills or stairs."

Linda had given up on dieting. She had tried various diets and experienced the ups and downs that plague many dieters. She was out of work too, so she was doing a lot of stress eating, scarfing down chocolate brownies with chocolate frosting. Linda was only in her early fifties but she had a lot of medical issues: fibromyalgia, systemic lupus, discoid lupus, chronic fatigue, high blood pressure, elevated sugar factor, and more.

One day, Linda was getting her hair done and started talking to the hairdresser, who had lost eighty-six pounds after having a gastric bypass. Linda knew that she didn't need something like that; her problem was simple: "just plain overeating." Her hairdresser agreed and told her to do the following three things, which Linda shares with us in her story:

"Number 1. Thank God for the body you have—every night and every day. Visualize the size you want to be and thank God for it. I wanted to be a size 10. I thanked God for making me a perfect size 10.

"Number 2. Eat anything you want—but eat off a cake plate, not a dinner plate. This is for breakfast, lunch and dinner. Eat slowly, appreciating every bite. No second helpings. Drink lots of water.

"Number 3. Get out and walk, walk, walk. I walk the local mall on Monday, Wednesday and Friday. It has two levels. By the time I have walked both levels I have broken a sweat."

Linda had been faithfully doing all three of those things for seven months by the time that she wrote her story. She had lost thirty-three pounds, but more importantly, her blood pressure was under control, her blood sugar was normal, and her lupus was in remission.

Her three pieces of advice are the same simple, wise ideas that Emme and Richard Simmons live by and have lovingly shared with countless others over the decades: *love it, nurture it, and use it.* Those are three tips that simplify what might otherwise be an overly complicated relationship with our bodies.

Pretend to Be the Person You Want to Be

And, miraculously, you will become that person

Sometimes I think it will say this on my tombstone: *They really fell for it.* And that's because there have been so many times I did something new, something that I wasn't sure I could do at all, and somehow pulled it off.

I think for many women that way of thinking starts with the first baby, when they put you in the wheelchair in the hospital, put the baby in your lap, and start wheeling you to the elevator. Inside you're saying, *Wait! Isn't there a test I'm supposed to take? Don't you know I have no idea how to take care of this totally dependent, helpless, fragile little creature?* But you head home and you fake it, and your baby thinks you're the greatest mom ever.

After that there are many other times you have to pretend. I remember when we first bought Chicken Soup for the Soul and I had to make an unbelievable, impossible, insane number of books in just six months: twenty-eight books, seven of them with new stories and twenty-one with my favorite stories from our library, on a wide range of topics, from dogs to raising kids to faith to golf and more. It was a crazy time but somehow we pulled it off and I went from being the biggest rookie in the publishing industry to one who had walked through fire and survived.

I love the fact that we get lots of Chicken Soup for the Soul stories about this, proving that much of success comes from acting as if you are already the person that everyone expects you to be. The more you act as that person *would* act, and do what that person *would* do, the more you will *become* that person.

***

One of my favorite stories about pretending to be the person you want to be is from *Chicken Soup for the Soul: Reboot Your Life*. In "The Life of the Party" Giulietta Nardone tells us that she was painfully shy, always the wallflower at social and business events. She would panic when she thought about saying *Hello, what do you do?* to a stranger.

> *Much of success comes from acting as if you are already the person that everyone expects you to be.*

I used to think that if you started out shy, you would be shy for life, but I've learned from our writers that shyness is a trait that can be changed. We often get stories from people who have consciously and deliberately overcome their shyness, and they are even confident and outgoing enough now to tell the rest of us, "Hey, I used to be shy and here's what I did to get over it."

Giulietta shares with us that her shyness not only made her feel isolated, it actually caused people to think that she was conceited and aloof, even cold. But she wasn't. She wanted to be friendly, but ever since a "classic mean girl" had bullied her in school she'd been afraid to put herself out there.

When Giulietta took a class called "How To Make Small Talk," she learned how to approach strangers and engage them in conversation. She practiced by talking to her reflection in the mirror.

She still hadn't conquered her fear of talking to strangers when she started her own graphic design company. Now she absolutely *had* to learn how to talk to strangers. She couldn't build a business otherwise. When she was invited to a political fundraiser around that time, she made a resolution. She would practice for real this time. She would force herself to talk to people she didn't know.

She gave herself a scary assignment — to talk to everyone in the room.

The day of the party, she sat in the parking lot in her car for fifteen minutes, willing herself to go in. Then she did it. She walked in and went right over to the first stranger she saw, extended her hand, and faked confidence. Giulietta acted the part of a non-shy, confident person and she talked to everyone in that room. They responded to her like this was a normal thing, which it *was* for them. She had a great time.

Giulietta says, "Surprisingly, the more I reached out to converse, the easier it got. I learned to ask questions that engaged the other person's interest or revealed common ground."

Before the evening was over, Giulietta was introducing people to each other! After all, she was talking to all of them, learning about them, so now she could facilitate them meeting each other. The shy girl had become a networker — a matchmaker. By the end of the evening, she says, "I felt powerful, connected and free."

That broke the ice for Giulietta. She started seeking out opportunities to start conversations. She realized those occasions were all around her. And the world became a kinder, warmer, and happier place for her. She was still shy, but she kept up the act — pretending to be a non-shy person. And eventually she became a non-shy person for real.

After five years of putting herself out there, she could walk up to anyone at any kind of event and start a conversation. Because she has become such a friendly person, her business has grown, and she has more friends than she ever imagined.

Giulietta knew she had made it when she heard a business acquaintance introduce her at a local networking group as "the woman who everyone knows in town." She had become that fun person who the old Giulietta wouldn't have had the courage to approach.

It sounds like something from a movie, right? Shy girl becomes the life of the party? But I've seen more than one Chicken Soup for the Soul story in which this strategy worked. It's worth thinking about.

***

This "act like the person you want to become" method really works! Here's another example, which Alisa Edwards Smith wrote for *Chicken Soup for the Soul: Thanks to My Mom*. The story is called "Fake It Till You Make It," a phrase that her mother lived by.

Alisa's mother was always a whirlwind of activity, making impossible things happen. Alisa tells us about the time when she was a kid and her mother was running an orphanage in Nigeria. She watched her mother pick up some of the concrete mixture that was being used to build a water tower for the orphans, and then tell the workmen, with absolute authority and confidence, "There is too much sand in this mixture."

The men all nodded at her mother's pronouncement and told her they would add the correct ingredients, and Alisa's mother strode away, satisfied.

When Alisa was alone with her mom, she said, "Mother, I didn't know that you knew anything about concrete."

"I don't!" her mother replied. "I just know that putting too much sand in the mixture is how they cheat you."

Alisa says her mother was a force of nature. She had grown up in the Appalachian Mountains in a house with no heat and no plumbing, and she was the first person in her family to graduate from high school. She had dreams and hopes way beyond her family's means: to go into medicine, marry a doctor and go to Africa. And she did just that, leading up to that day when she strode fearlessly into that group of men and supervised the building of something she knew nothing about.

When Alisa was frightened on her first day of classes at Duke University, she channeled her mother. When she was nervous about raising her children — which, frankly, none of us knows how to do until we've already done it — Alisa channeled her mother. No matter what challenges arose, no matter how Alisa had to stretch to try new things, she remembered her mother's mantra: "Fake it till you make it."

***

Mary Wood Bridgman's mother had another great saying, which is the title of Mary's story, "Tell Them You Can Do It," in the same *Thanks to My Mom* book. Mary's mother was a teacher and she took on interns every year. One day, Mary's mom told her intern, who was preparing for an interview, "Whatever

> "Tell them you can do it."

they want you to do, you tell them you can do it." Whether it was math or geography or home economics, her mom told the intern, "Tell them you can do it."

Mary earned a law degree and went to work for a law firm. For the first five years of her career, she felt woefully ill-equipped to handle just about anything that crossed her desk. She found transaction work painstaking and confusing, and courtroom appearances scary and intimidating, but she kept that to herself. She kept following the advice that her mother gave to that intern, telling her bosses that she could do whatever they asked her to do.

Later, Mary became an expert in a number of new fields when she took a corporate job. There was no one else to do it, so she did. She was given more and more responsibility, and kept on stretching beyond her comfort zone, never turning down new responsibilities. If they asked, she said she could do it, and then she figured out how. Mary still lives by her mother's words, no matter how tired, intimidated or overwhelmed she feels: "Tell them you can do it."

***

Making TV and radio appearances has always been part of my career, but there were times when I didn't know what I was doing, and had to use the "fake it till you make it" and "tell them you can do it" mantras to make it happen.

As a Wall Street analyst covering a hot industry — and as a younger, blonder, cuter model of analyst than most of my stodgy, older, male competitors — I was interviewed a lot on television. Of course, I also knew my stuff, and I wasn't afraid to take an investment stance that was controversial. It wasn't unusual to have a film crew traipsing onto our floor at my brokerage firm to interview me about the latest developments in telecommunications. Those interviews lasted a few minutes and before I knew it they were over. I don't even remember the first one, but I'm sure it was on FNN (Financial News Network), which ended up merging with today's CNBC — because I went on that channel a lot.

One TV appearance from those days stands out, however; I was invited to appear on Maryland Public Broadcasting's *Wall $treet Week*. This was *huge*. Going on W$W was the *pinnacle* for an analyst and most never got to do it. The producer told me I would be the youngest featured guest they'd ever had.

I had been working like a dog for months, preparing for the breakup of AT&T into eight new publicly traded companies, which would occur on January 1, 1984. My job on the December 23, 1983 show would be to explain the breakup and advise viewers on what to do with the eight new stocks they would get in place of good old, reliable Ma Bell.

Of course, I did myself in. A couple of days before the appearance I was so sick that I could barely get out of bed. My first-husband-to-be Phil got me on the train to Baltimore and delivered me to the television studio. I tried to fake being healthy, but I was practically delirious with fever and my throat was so sore that uttering any sound at all was agonizing.

The crew poured honey and tea down my throat a few minutes before the taping, in hopes I'd be able to get some kind of rasping sound to come out. They said their concoction should give me a working voice for about half an hour.

Then I sat behind a wall on the set, trying not to pass out, waiting for the introductory part of the show to end. Someone would usher me out to the couches to opine on the AT&T breakup with the Wall Street experts assembled there.

That's when I heard a crashing sound.

Part of the set had fallen over.

"This never happens," the crew told me as they rushed to put it back together. The extra time it would take them to fix it meant we now had to do the show *live*. And they'd have to pour that vile mixture down my throat one more time to try to resurrect my voice again!

When the cameras started rolling for real, I gathered every ounce of energy I had, sat up straight, smiled at the host, and pretended both the set and I were sturdy and strong. Even though every word I uttered felt like swallowing broken glass, for fifteen minutes I pretended to be a non-feverish, able-voiced expert on a magnificent set... and the six million viewers were none the wiser. I even got a couple of marriage proposals in the fan mail that came in after the show.

Of course, I collapsed as soon as the director yelled, "Cut." But hey, that's showbiz. Fake it till you make it.

I was sick in bed for the next three weeks, even missing Christmas and New Year's.

Where I was truly at a loss, though, was when I appeared on QVC twenty-five years later to sell our books. QVC is like a parallel universe, and the whole experience, which lasted a few months, still seems surreal to me.

The first thing you do is make the pilgrimage to QVC headquarters in West Chester, Pennsylvania to pitch your product. The place is mammoth and impressively professional and filled with hopeful entrepreneurs and manufacturers, all praying that QVC will bless them with a "yes."

We got a "yes" and I was appointed our on-air spokesperson. The next step was to return for an all-day training session to learn how to sell, QVC-style.

The night before the boot camp, I stayed at a nearby Sheraton, which was an experience in itself. I'd venture to say that 99% of the hotel guests were visiting QVC. All of the numerous TVs in the lobby were tuned to QVC. Every person I saw in that lobby looked nervous and hopeful at the same time. There were men wheeling around heavy carts loaded with newfangled consumer products, heavily made-up women returning from their appearances looking exhausted and relieved, business partners consulting with each other in urgent but hushed voices before their presentations. We were part of one gigantic twenty-four-hour selling machine.

Two weeks after my training session, I was back at QVC to make my first appearance.

They did my make-up and I was taken through a door into a huge, confusing world of stage sets. It was so big that you had to be driven in a golf cart if you were going to one of the farther out stages.

And then came the moment of truth. On every TV show I had ever done, the rule was very clear: "Do not look at the camera."

Guests always look at hosts and cameras are positioned to show the guests talking to the hosts.

You *never* look at the camera — *ever.*

But on QVC you *have* to look at the camera to connect with the viewers. They taught us this.

But which one? When I stepped onto the set, I saw three.

"You'll see a red light glowing on the camera you're sup-posed to look at. That's the only one that's on at any given time," a crewmember told me. Here's the catch: The host could see all three cameras from her seat, but from mine, which was angled to talk to the host, I could see only *one.*

"No problem," I said. After all, I had done this before many times. In front of millions of people.

But a minute later there I was, turning my gaze away from the host as we went live, frantically trying to find the one camera out of three that was "on." I must have looked downright shifty, furtively looking around as I tried to find that red light. Every time I found it, it would change and I'd have to find it all over again on another camera.

I was invited back on QVC two more times after that, so maybe I pulled it off, but I'm not sure. I definitely didn't master that one!

Those "fake it till you make it" and "tell them you can do it" strategies might not work perfectly 100% of the time, but for me, they work *almost* all the time. I wouldn't have done half the things I've done if I hadn't said *yes* first and then figured out *how* later.

* * *

Tell them you can do it, like lawyer Mary Bridgman, even when it's new and scary. Pretend you have X-ray vision like Alisa's mom and you know exactly what's inside that murky concrete mixture. Fake confidence at a party until you actually have some, like Giulietta.

You'll be the only one in on the secret.

Expect Great Things of People

You'll be amazed how they will rise to the challenge

ere's the great news: You can apply what you learned in Chapter 6 to *other* people, too! I talked about how you can pretend to be what you want to be, and somehow you will become that person. You can also "pretend" that other people will do things that they weren't necessarily expecting to do, and sure enough, they will come through! They might even do things they thought were impossible.

If you treat people as if they are capable or willing, no matter what you are asking of them, you'll find they will very often do what you need them to do. This works on your children, your colleagues, and on perfect strangers.

People will rise to your expectations and even surprise themselves. I've also discovered that if you ask someone to do something for you that is not *ordinarily* done, and you act as if it is a foregone conclusion they *will* do it, they almost always will!

For example, one recent afternoon I was walking our son Tim's Shiba Inu, Charlie, who was staying with us for a couple of months while Tim was on location making a film. I really wanted coffee so I poked my head in the door of the cute little Starbucks building across the street from our office and called in to the barista, saying, "Hi, I'm not allowed to bring in a dog, right?" He confirmed that Charlie was not welcome. "Okay, well since it's not busy and there's no one in line, can you come and get my iPhone from me and make me a tall soy misto and use the app on my phone to pay for it?"

He looked surprised, but then I saw him thinking something like... *Okay, this is not an unreasonable request, and even though this customer is asking me for something I have never done before, I can do this.* He came and got my phone and brought it back to me with my coffee a few minutes later.

***

This strategy has worked for me my whole life. I always act as if I'm sure people will do things for me, and I'm almost never disappointed.

I first learned that people will do things for you if you let them when I was doing the research for my college thesis in Brazil. I was traveling the Amazon Highway by bus, meeting with poets and writers and collecting their stories. I was studying a particular kind of popular literature that was unique to the poverty-stricken northeast of Brazil and the people in that community went out of their way to help the twenty-year-old *pesquisadora americana* (American researcher). They introduced me to the right people, gave me their own copies of out-of-print books, and helped me in every possible way.

For two months, I led a charmed life. Whatever I needed would materialize when I needed it. I got used to it! If you're open to things working out, and you present this attitude to the world, it's remarkable how things will come together for you.

What I got from that time in Brazil was invaluable. It set me up for everything that was to come, giving me faith in my own abilities and the kindness of strangers, teaching me inner strength and resilience, and training me in the art of speaking to strangers and asking for their stories. And who knew that after collecting stories *from the people* in Brazil, I would end up doing the same thing thirty years later at Chicken Soup for the Soul? That's one of those funny coincidences that hadn't even occurred to me until after I started this job.

That Brazil experience has never left me—I continue to believe that good things will happen if you let them. So when my twenty-year-old son Michael got a grant to go to Mallorca one summer to do a research project on a famous painter named Miquel Barceló, I knew the same thing would happen to him.

> *"People will help you and it will all magically come together."*

I was driving Mike to JFK to catch his flight to Spain and he was saying that he wasn't even sure where he was going to stay when he got to Mallorca. I told him that everything would work out, just as it had for me at the same age when I was traveling around Brazil.

"Just *expect* things to work," I said. "People will help you and it will all magically come together." And that's what happened for Mike. He found a great place to stay for the whole summer, renting a room from one of Barceló's childhood friends; he was able to talk to everyone in Barceló's circle; and anyone he wanted to meet welcomed him.

At the end of the summer, Mike was sitting with a friend of Barceló's one day in Barcelona, and the guy said, "I'm calling Miquel. He has to know you." When Barceló picked up, he said to his friend, "Who is this American kid who is talking to everyone I know?" The guy handed the phone to Mike: "Talk to Miquel," he said.

The next thing Mike knew he was talking to the most famous painter in Spain and was invited to meet him in Geneva at the opening ceremony for a dome Barceló had painted for the UN. This led to Mike living in Barceló's studio in Paris for several months the next year and traveling all over Europe and West Africa with him. All that good stuff culminated in Mike writing a bestselling book about his time with Barceló and about Barceló's life.

As predicted, magic happened.

***

I know people say that putting on rose-colored glasses is a bad thing, but I don't agree. Sometimes putting on rose-colored glasses doesn't only make things *look* rosy — it changes them for real!

Jennie Ivey, one of our regular writers, illustrates this in her story called "The Honors Class," from *Chicken Soup for the Soul: The Power of Positive.*

Jennie was a first-year teacher so she was excited that she had been chosen to teach an honors-level U.S. history class. Usually new teachers didn't get the honors classes.

But Jennie was assigned an honors class during first period. In preparation for the eager learners she expected, she decorated the classroom with Presidential portraits, colorful maps and framed copies of the Declaration of Independence and the Constitution. When the kids shuffled in unenthusiastically the first day, she figured that was just how high school kids were.

"I'm so excited to have been selected to teach this class," she told them. "We're going to do things a little differently in this class because I know that all of you want a challenge."

When the kids stared at her, dumbfounded by her perky enthusiasm, she soldiered on, rearranging their desks in a circle so they could have class discussions.

Then she asked the kids to explain what they *didn't* like about history class.

"Amanda hated how history seemed to be all about war," Jennie said. "José didn't like memorizing names and dates. Gerald was convinced that nothing that had happened in the past was relevant to his life. 'Why should I care about a bunch of dead white guys?' was how he put it. Caitlyn hated tricky true-false questions. Miranda despised fill-in-the-blank tests."

Armed with that feedback, Jennie made a plan. She wouldn't teach from the textbook. She wouldn't make them read a chapter and then take a quiz. She wouldn't limit their topics to generals and battles. Instead, she would explore social and economic history and tie in current events to make the past feel relevant to their lives today. Jennie bubbled over with ideas to appeal to these kids, with their higher-level skills.

People will rise to your expectations and even surprise themselves.

"We'd read novels to bring home the humanity of history. *Across Five Aprils* when studying the Civil War. *The Grapes of Wrath* to learn about the Great Depression. *The Things They Carried* when talking about Vietnam."

After all, these kids were bright and motivated. Jennie says, "My honors class deserved to be taught in a way that would speak to them."

Jennie was surprised by how many of her students used poor grammar and lacked writing skills, but they were, after all, in one of the rougher high schools in her area. She knew they were great kids and treated them as such, with the result being that many of the kids were not only willing, but eager, to attend after-school study sessions.

Four of Jennie's students even formed their own "History Bowl" team and entered a countywide history contest. They were ecstatic when they won an Honorable Mention trophy.

The school year came to an end more quickly than Jennie could have imagined. When she thought back over the year, she couldn't help it — it was the kids in her honors class who were her favorites. She was so lucky to have gotten that class her first year. No one had averaged lower than a C and most had gotten A's and B's.

On the final day before summer break, Jennie's principal called her in for her end-of-year evaluation. "I want to congratulate you on a great rookie season," she said. "Especially on how well you did with your remedial kids."

Jennie was confused. She didn't have any remedial classes.

The principal pulled out the roster for Jennie's first period class from a file folder and handed it to her, saying, "Your first period class was remedial. Surely you saw that indicated at the top of the roll."

She went on to say that Jennie must have noticed the kids' poor reading and writing skills. "And you must have suspected the students in that class were below average by the way they dressed and the way they carried themselves."

Jennie looked at the class list. There at the top, printed plain as day, was the word "HONORS."

She showed it to the principal.

"Oh, dear," the principal said. "What a huge mistake! How did you ever manage, treating slow students as though they were…?"

Jennie knew how that sentence was going to end, so she finished it herself.

"As though they were bright?"

The principal nodded, sheepishly. The "mistake" was a big lesson for that principal, and for a first-year teacher who saw a class of remedial kids through rose-colored glasses and turned it into a class of motivated learners after all.

Before their meeting was over, the principal circled the word HONORS at the top of the class roster and put it back in its file folder.

"Next year, I may just have this printed at the top of all the class rolls."

It was a lesson that neither of those educators would ever forget.

CHAPTER
8

Be Bold and Speak Out

Act on your instincts even if it's embarrassing or inconvenient

The first time I remember my big mouth getting me in real trouble was when I was a senior in high school. My English teacher, Mr. Davis, had made a pronouncement one day early in the first semester.

"In this classroom," he warned us, "you may *not* use the words 'symbolism' or 'symbolic.' Ever!" I thought his rule to banish those words was not only ridiculous, but illogical. If Mr. Davis was worried about us using the terms incorrectly, why not teach us how to use them properly instead?

Shortly thereafter, we read a poem in class and I raised my hand. "Mr. Davis, I know that we're not allowed to use the word 'symbolism' so what word should we use to describe this poem?" And I pointed out a particularly symbolic portion of the poem. I did not ask this in a rude way; I was merely confused and looking for guidance.

Mr. Davis looked at me with contempt. "You," he said, pointing at me and then at the door. "Get out of my classroom. *And don't come back.*"

He was serious. The room was silent as I gathered my books and left, bewildered and red-faced. Even though I had only used the offensive word to ask *a question* about using it — still, I had technically committed the crime and was now banned from his English class. *For life.*

Mr. Davis was the head of the English Department and he

decreed that no other English teacher could take me in, juvenile delinquent that I was. For the next three weeks, I hung out with my friends during my new free period, and then reality set in. I wasn't going to graduate from high school. The New York State requirement was four years of English class and I only had three.

That's when my mother pointed out to the principal that I had not exactly *committed a felony* by saying *that word*. The next afternoon, I was sent to a new, fearless English teacher, *on probation*. And I spent the rest of the year happily devouring majestic novels by Tolstoy and Dostoevsky and writing essays with lots of naughty words like "symbolism," "metaphor," and "simile."

I never regretted what I did. But I did learn an important lesson. Speaking out can be lonely. Several of my classmates approached me after the Mr. Davis incident to praise me for speaking up in class, but not one of them had the courage to stand up with me against him. Imagine what would have happened if the whole class had objected. He couldn't very well have kicked out all of us, and perhaps he would have changed his ways for future students.

***

One of my favorite stories for our teenage readers is about another girl who spoke up in class. She even got an apology from *her* teacher. The story is called "Speaking Up" and we published it in *Chicken Soup for the Soul: Just for Teenagers.*

Alexis Streb started out like many other teenagers. She didn't do mean things herself, but when she saw kids making fun of the students who were "different," she didn't intervene.

Then her little brother was diagnosed with autism, and Alexis's whole family got involved with helping him, even moving and changing schools more than once so he could get the proper kind of help.

Alexis became much more knowledgeable about kids with

handicaps or learning disabilities. She was still afraid to intervene in any major way, though, when she saw bullies making fun of the kids who had school aides or other obvious differences. One day, she even saw some kids making fun of the students who were getting on what the kids rudely called the "short bus" in the bus line next to theirs. Alexis said something about it, quietly, but no one listened and she didn't push it. She says she immediately regretted not saying more.

Then, one day, when Alexis was at yet another new school, she was at band practice and the teacher said this to the band: "Guys, we're playing like the kids on the short bus! Come on!"

Alexis couldn't believe an adult had said this. The entire room was laughing when she raised her hand. Alexis's face turned bright red. She was the new kid and she was about to tell off a teacher!

You have to listen to your gut and be willing to speak up, even when it's embarrassing or inconvenient.

But she *did* it, saying, "I don't think we should make fun of the 'short bus,' because there are a lot of people on that bus who have great personalities and have the same feelings we do. And also, I know some people on those buses and they are some of the most caring, sweetest, and smartest people so I would appreciate it if you didn't make fun of them."

The teacher immediately apologized. Alexis got some stares from the other kids, but she felt good. She says, "While everyone in the classroom was being a follower, I had decided to take a different path."

There are so many times we keep quiet and then regret it later. Alexis learned a valuable lesson about speaking up for your convictions and for what's right. And she felt great that she had done it. After all, if you don't have pride in your own actions, if you feel like a little mouse who goes with the crowd, how can you feel good about yourself? The fact is that you have to listen to your gut and be willing to speak up, even when it's embarrassing or inconvenient. You're not only doing it to help other people—you're doing it to help yourself, too.

***

Without boring you with all the details, suffice it to say that majoring in Portuguese in college did not lead to any spectacular job offers. Therefore, I pursued one of my other passions, telecommunications, and ended up on Wall Street a couple of years after graduation, following telecom stocks. That job, as a stock analyst, was terrific, because I was able to keep doing it part-time from home as a freelancer when I started having babies.

I was known for being very honest about my stock recommendations. If I thought that a stock would go down instead of up, I would say so, even though that didn't always make me popular. When you're talking about people's money—their stock market wins or losses—things get pretty testy. And boy did I test a lot of people, because I never took anything at face value. If a company said that it was doing well, I wanted proof. Did its customers really like its products? Would they keep buying them? Was the company being totally honest with investors?

One of my specialties was figuring out when companies were defrauding investors by overstating how well they were doing. The worst case of this was when I discovered that a telephone equipment manufacturer named Intellicall was faking its revenues. They were pretending to sell lots of newfangled phone equipment to their customers, but they were actually stashing millions of dollars worth of the stuff in a warehouse that I found by doing some detective work, plus they were shipping equipment to customers who hadn't actually ordered it. Imagine coming into work one morning and finding your office filled with big boxes of phone gear that you hadn't ordered, because the company that shipped it wanted to count more sales on their financial statements.

It was a major accounting fraud, and I opened my big mouth and told people. The company fought back and continued to mislead their accountants. They got away with it for a whole extra year after I "outed" them. But even their accountants finally saw through the fake sales, and the top management team was fired. Right before they were fired, though, they took their revenge on me, and filed a lawsuit blaming me for the fact that their stock price plummeted. So there I was, a part-time analyst, full-time mother of two toddlers — the first analyst in history ever sued by a New York Stock Exchange company.

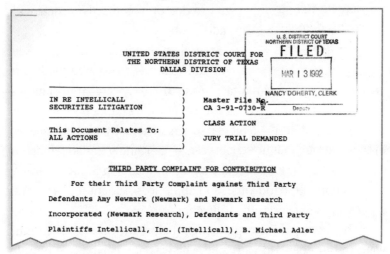

UNITED STATES DISTRICT COURT FOR
THE NORTHERN DISTRICT OF TEXAS
DALLAS DIVISION

U. S. DISTRICT COURT
NORTHERN DISTRICT OF TEXAS

FILED

MAR 1 3 1992

NANCY DOHERTY, CLERK

IN RE INTELLICALL   )   Master File No.
SECURITIES LITIGATION   )   CA 3-91-0730-R   Deputy
)
)   CLASS ACTION
This Document Relates To:)
ALL ACTIONS   )   JURY TRIAL DEMANDED
)

THIRD PARTY COMPLAINT FOR CONTRIBUTION

For their Third Party Complaint against Third Party

Defendants Amy Newmark (Newmark) and Newmark Research

Incorporated (Newmark Research), Defendants and Third Party

Plaintiffs Intellicall, Inc. (Intellicall), B. Michael Adler

Terrifying. And expensive. I was being sued for millions of dollars and I had to hire lawyers to defend me. Those were some anxious times.

I was vindicated in the end. When I finally got to speak my piece during my deposition and share my twenty-five single-spaced pages of evidence, the Intellicall lawyer was horrified. The poor guy had no idea his client was so guilty and he did something unheard of — he apologized and dropped the case against me. *And,* he made Intellicall pay all my legal expenses.

* * *

One of my favorite role models for speaking up and making a difference is Ginger Katz. I met Ginger and her husband Larry a few years ago and I asked them to share their story in *Chicken Soup for the Soul: Find Your Inner Strength*. Ginger's story is called "A Mother's Promise to Her Son" and it's about the worst thing imaginable — finding her twenty-year-old son dead of a drug overdose the morning that he was planning to go to a doctor, voluntarily, to deal with his addiction.

> *"Not everything that is faced can be changed, but nothing can be changed until it is faced."*

The doctor advised Ginger to lie about Ian's death — to say that he died of an aneurysm or a heart attack. After all, they were an upstanding middle-class family — drug overdoses didn't happen to them. Ian was a good kid, too — a bit of a superstar actually. He had excelled in sports throughout his school years — captaining teams, competing as a black belt in karate at age eleven in Madison Square Garden. He was popular, handsome, and an honors student too. This was a kid who had everything to live for.

Ginger couldn't sleep the night before the funeral. She didn't want to bury her son with a lie. She was not ashamed of him. In fact, she had a vision of herself speaking out. She woke up her husband and said that she wanted to tell everyone — that this could happen in their families too — and she wanted to work to stop this. That morning she spoke the truth about Ian's death at his funeral.

"They say the truth will set you free, and I believe it," says Ginger. "Once I made the decision to be honest about Ian's addiction, I became the strong one at the funeral."

Ginger educated herself about addiction. She took classes, attended seminars, read research. Then she approached the principal of Ian's high school in Norwalk, Connecticut and arranged to tell his story to the students there.

Now Ginger shares Ian's story across the country with students, parents, educators, law enforcement, and at state and national conferences. Ginger lives near me in Connecticut so I see her in the news all the time.

I know we are hearing more about drug addiction today—including in families like Ginger's that used to keep it a secret, but Ian died almost twenty years ago, when the subject was way more taboo. I think that Ginger's outspokenness, then and now, has contributed to the more open dialogue we are seeing about drug use—ending the shame so that families in all sectors of society can seek help, or, better yet, recognize the danger signs and stop drug use before it even starts.

Ginger's organization is called The Courage to Speak Foundation, because it was that courage to speak at the funeral that started all this. Ginger says, "I made a promise to Ian the day he died to do everything in my power to prevent this tragedy from happening to another family. I never thought this would happen in our family, but it did. Addiction crosses all age ranges, economic and ethnic backgrounds and races, and I will never stop speaking out until I see changes in our world."

The great American writer James Baldwin said, "Not everything that is faced can be changed, but nothing can be changed until it is faced." Ginger faced up to Ian's death with courage and conviction, and I am positive that she has saved many lives as a result.

***

Alexis and Ginger both spoke out on behalf of people who needed help. But how about when you have a gut feeling, a premonition, or some kind of urge to voice a protest, issue a warning, or stop something from happening? That can be *so* embarrassing. Everyone thinks you're crazy. I say, "Go for it." After all, you don't want to be saying "if only" because you *didn't* speak up. (You'll hear more about the words "if only" in the next chapter.)

James Gemmell spoke up, not only to his boss, but to his boss's boss, and his boss's boss's boss. And it was worth it. He tells us his story in *Chicken Soup for the Soul: Hope & Miracles* in "Small Voice, Big Message."

James was a new electrician in a paper mill, working with guys who had been there for years. One of his co-workers, Fred, was in charge, as he had been working at the mill more than fifteen years.

Since James had only been there two weeks, everything was new and interesting, and he was excited when he learned they would be having a "maintenance day." The equipment, which normally ran twenty-four hours a day, would be shut down for one eight-hour shift so the electricians could inspect it and make any repairs that were needed. And — very cool for James — that day they would be inspecting a bank of 2,200-volt electrical controllers.

That's a lot of voltage. If you touched one of those while it was on, you'd fry instantly. So there was a safety procedure. The powerhouse operator would lock down that voltage — make it dead.

James and his experienced, opinionated boss Fred gathered their tools and waited for the "all clear" from the powerhouse operator, telling them the voltage was off and they could touch those 2,200-volt electrical controllers.

The foreman arrived and said they were good to go. And even though James knew nothing, and was supposed to be quiet and obedient, a little voice in his head told him to speak up and demand absolute confirmation that the power had been shut off. He didn't want to be a jerk — after all he was brand-new — but he couldn't shake this feeling of foreboding. James demanded that someone do a voltage test to make sure the power was truly off.

Now he was in trouble. The only voltage tester was two kilometers away in another mill. There was a standoff — newbie know-nothing electrician James against his direct boss, his boss's boss, and his boss's boss's boss.

But for some reason, all those senior guys gave in. It took hours but they got the tester from the other mill.

James was probably going to lose his new job. When James's boss's boss's boss finally got back with the voltage tester, he was not happy. He was sweating, he was aggravated, and now they were late. He touched the voltage tester to the wire, ready to show the young whippersnapper not to question authority ever again.

The voltage tester lit up like a Christmas tree! The wires were completely live, not shut down at all. Everyone was speechless.

Here's how James describes what happened next: "The Chief walked over to me, his red face quickly turning white, and bear-hugged me, all the while muttering, 'Oh God, oh God.' The foreman approached me, shook my hand and in a voice full of emotion said that he had never been so happy to have one of his orders disobeyed. Fred, who seemed to have been hedging his bets up to that point, took over the situation from the two stunned supervisors and demanded that we all pay a visit to the powerhouse and get to the bottom of the lockout failure."

James says he has no idea where that little voice came from, but he knows it saved his life. He says it has never happened again, but if it ever does, he won't hesitate to listen to it.

Guess What You Can Accomplish in One Minute

Those small bits of time can change your life

Let's talk about minutes. We all live one minute at a time. And you can change your life with those "one minutes." Even if you only apply the tips in this chapter to *one* minute a day, life will be different for you.

Let me first acknowledge that I am a procrastinator. I'm the person who hates to hang up her clothing, the one who leaves that thing in the car for two weeks because it's a pain to open the lift gate and get it out.

I've fought that tendency my whole life — the tendency to put off those little tasks. But those little tasks weigh you down. You end up spending more time thinking about them, seeing them out of the corner of your eye, telling someone "No, I haven't done that yet," than if you just *did* them!

There are so many things you *don't* want to do that take only *one* minute! Here are a few examples:

- You can do that stretch that you're supposed to do after you exercise, the one you never have time for. Even if you only stretch for one minute, you'll feel it working. In fact, when you're in the middle of one of the harder stretches, and holding a challenging position, you'll be astounded by how long those sixty seconds will actually last!

- You can empty one whole rack of the dishwasher. And then you can take a second minute to do the other rack... or you can keep pretending the dishwasher hasn't been run and hope that someone else will empty it.

- You can clean out the vegetable drawer and throw away all that rotten produce that you bought two weeks ago when you were *really truly* going to make some salads and some healthy dinners with fruits and vegetables covering half the plate as recommended by the U.S. Department of Agriculture.

- You can put away that suitcase that has been sitting out there since your last trip. You and your spouse can ignore that suitcase for weeks, but I bet it will only take *half* a minute to put it away.

- You can get that thing out of the car that you keep leaving there. Or put your new insurance card — the one that's been sitting on the kitchen desk waiting to get lost — in the glove compartment.

- You can put away the clothes that you wore for the last three days. Somehow it seems like such a burden to hang them up at the end of the day, but it takes literally seconds to carry a sweater to the closet, put it on a hanger, and get it back where it belongs.

So set the timer on your phone. If you don't know how to do that, take one minute and find out how. Google it: "How do I set the timer on my iPhone/Android/Samsung" or whatever you have.

Or come up with your own trick, your own way of convincing yourself to do those little one-minute tasks.

This way you get rid of all the little things that are getting in the way of doing the big things. You spend way more time thinking about the fact that you have to do them than you would spend if you took a minute here and there and did them.

You can also entertain yourself while you do those one-minute tasks — for example, you could carry your cell phone or your iPad around with you and listen to a podcast or an audiobook while you're performing your one-minute chores.

***

Besides thinking about the things that I can get done in one minute, I have also been thinking a lot about those little packages of minutes that we waste. Maybe you have five minutes in the car before your kid emerges from school, or ten minutes in your office before your next appointment, or fifteen minutes every day on the subway.

I've always been impressed by the way my husband uses every minute of the day to accomplish things. Even if he only has a few minutes between appointments, he turns to his computer and does a project or he picks up something and reads it. Those minutes add up and I have been trying to follow his example, working on my books and my podcast scripts even when I only have little bits of time available.

> *If you regain only two percent of the minutes in your day by being mindful and not wasting them, you'll actually get back half an hour a day.*

I found several people with this admirable trait in *Chicken Soup for the Soul: Inspiration for Writers*. That makes sense because writing is very self-directed. As a writer, you have to be disciplined and sit down and get the job done. It's certainly something I've confronted while writing this book, which kept slipping to the back burner while other projects with more immediate deadlines jumped ahead on my to-do list.

One of our very prolific writers, Diane Stark, talked about this process in her story called "A Few Short Minutes." Diane had an epiphany one day when she was watching football. She writes, "A touchdown is nothing more than getting the ball across the field, yard by precious yard. Sometimes it happens in one amazing, record-setting pass. Other times, it occurs more slowly — just a few yards at a time." But six points are still six points.

> *"Much may be done in those little shreds and patches of time which every day produces, and which most men throw away."*

Diane says, "I thought about all the little blocks of time in my life that I thought were too short to use. I realized they were too long to waste. My life circumstances don't provide me with many big chunks of time to write. So I needed to use the small chunks productively."

She started writing a few minutes at a time, and reported, "Finally, minute by minute, word by word, I was writing. I was submitting my work and getting it accepted. It was my own personal end zone, and it felt nothing less than amazing."

Anna Redsand had another story on the same theme in our writing book. "The Man in the Green Pickup" was about a man who wrote in his truck every day during his lunch break. He only had fifteen minutes left by the time he finished eating, but he diligently wrote on a yellow legal pad, and after two years he had written a book and found a publisher.

This motivated Anna, a single mother working full-time as a school counselor, to write the inspirational book for teens she had in mind. She realized that she had a twenty-minute window of opportunity every morning before she left for work. That was five minutes more than the man in the green truck.

According to Anna, "Those twenty minutes a day turned me into the writer I am today." It took her two years to complete her book, *Viktor Frankl: A Life Worth Living*, but she did. It was published by Clarion Books.

The English writer Charles Caleb Colton said, "Much may be done in those little shreds and patches of time which every day produces, and which most men throw away."

I think that holds true for all our endeavors, not just writing.

Do the math. If you regain only *two percent* of the minutes in your day by being mindful and not wasting them, you'll actually get back *half an hour a day* of usable time.

***

There's one more aspect of minutes that I want to discuss: taking the extra minute to do things right. Why? Because two of the saddest words in the English language are "if only."

I hate the words "if only" and I live my life with the goal of never having to say them. They convey regret, lost opportunities, mistakes, and disappointment. And sometimes the words "if only" go along with terrible tragedies. Think about how many times you have heard about something awful happening, accompanied by "if only he had called her back to make sure she was okay…" or "if only I had investigated that noise…" or "if only they had made sure the gate to the pool clicked behind them…"

The English jurist Edward Coke said, "Precaution is better than cure." And my father-in-law, Bill Senior, was famous in our family for saying, "Take the extra minute to do it right." He must have done something right, since he lived to age ninety-one and was "all there" right to the end.

I always try to live by the "extra minute" rule. Sometimes it only takes seconds to make sure I write something down correctly, or check something on the Internet, or move an object out of the way before it trips someone. And, of course, when my children were young, and prone to all kinds of mishaps, I lived and breathed the extra minute rule. I always thought about what I could do to avoid an "if only" moment, whether it was something minor like moving a cup full of hot coffee away from the edge of a counter, or something that required a little more work such as taping padding onto the sharp corners of a glass coffee table.

I remember reading a news story about a student pilot who was thrown from an airplane when its canopy lifted off. The instructor, who was belted in, was fine. The student, whose seatbelt was not fastened, fell from the sky. Imagine how many people are in mourning, and how terrified that man must have been as he fell from the plane. Imagine the chorus of "if only" coming from his family. If only he had been wearing his seatbelt... How simple would that have been?

I don't move my car one inch until I hear the seatbelt click on every passenger. I unplug the iron when I leave the laundry room for "just a minute." I'd hate to get distracted, not return to the laundry room, and start a fire with that forgotten iron. Imagine the "if only" I'd be saying then. After I realized that I could not be trusted with a teakettle — I left it boiling on the stove for an hour — I threw out its burned carcass and bought an electric teakettle that shuts itself off. And I am paranoid about fireplace ashes. I wait till they are two weeks old, then shovel them into a bag on garbage collection day and put the bag twenty feet away from the house in the middle of the driveway.

When my teenage son was first driving, I worried that enforcing his curfew too strictly would cause him to speed and have an accident. A boy in the next town was killed when he drove too fast trying to make it home by midnight. So my son and I agreed on a plan — if he missed curfew he would just lose double those minutes the next night out. Ten minutes late meant twenty minutes shaved off the curfew the next time, consequences that were not so onerous that they would cause him to rush home.

I don't only avoid those "if only" moments when it comes to safety. It's equally important to avoid "if only" in our personal relationships. We all know people who lost a loved one and bemoaned the fact that they had foregone an opportunity to say "I love you" or "I forgive you."

When my father announced he was going to the eye doctor across from my office on Good Friday, I told him that it was a holiday for Chicken Soup for the Soul and I wouldn't be there. But then I thought about the fact that he was in his mid-eighties and I realized that I shouldn't give up an opportunity to see him. I called him and told him I had decided to go to work on my day off after all.

When my husband's beloved, elderly uncle pocket-dialed me several times with his new cell phone, I urged my husband to call him back, invoking the "if only" possibility. My husband called him and was glad that he did.

I know there will still be occasions when I have to say "if only" about something, but my life is definitely more serene because of my policy of doing everything possible to avoid that eventuality. And even though it takes an extra minute to do something right, or it occasionally takes an hour or two in my busy schedule to make a personal connection, I know that I'm doing the right thing. I'm buying myself peace of mind and that's the best kind of insurance for my emotional wellbeing.

***

Life is short so why waste one minute of it? In fact, why does anyone ever say they want to "kill" time when so many of us wish we had more of it… when it rushes through our fingers like sand slipping away in an hourglass? You can find precious, lost time throughout your day and use it to get dozens of important little tasks done or even one great accomplishment, bit by bit. And with the minutes you get back by being efficient, you can do what my father-in-law advised and "take the extra minute to do it right."

Because you'll find that it's the little bits of time that add up to make a lifetime's worth of difference.

Find Your Happy

How to bring purpose and passion into your life

We all want to be happy, and I've given a lot of thought to what our writers have taught us about the successful pursuit of happiness. Here are seven key tips that I've gleaned from thousands of people who have found their own paths to having happy lives:

1. **Pursue at least one of your passions.**

   If you have a job that you only do to pay the bills, then that is your job, but it doesn't have to be what you *do*. Find some time to do what you actually love doing. I've heard that you should think back to your favorite activities when you were ten years old and try to do those now. For me, it was two things: reading, and hiking in the woods behind our house. And now I do just that — I read for work, I read for pleasure, and when weather and time permit, my husband and I go hiking on the trails in the nature preserve in our neighborhood.

2. **Do something that has meaning to you and gives you purpose.**

   Ralph Waldo Emerson said, "Make yourself necessary to

somebody." You lift yourself when you lift others. We have hundreds of stories from people who found that doing some kind of volunteer work practically saved their lives — it turned everything around for them to be giving back and to feel valued by other people, no matter what their own circumstances. Doing *good* for others is incredibly *good* for you.

3. Count your blessings.

We get more stories than we could possibly publish from people who have purposefully turned their attitudes around by keeping a journal. Some people write down one good thing that happened to them each day, even if it's something like "there was no line at the bank this morning." Other people make themselves write down three good things that happen to them each day. It may sound hokey but it works. It's been scientifically proven that people who keep track of the "good things" in their lives are healthier and more productive, and they get along better with other people.

4. Smile at everyone.

No matter what kind of day you are having, smile. I talked about this at length in Chapter 2. It works even if you're having a bad day! If you smile at people, they will smile back at you and it will change your day.

5. Keep learning.

Have you ever noticed how energized you feel when you learn something new? Of course, you are already doing that by reading this book! My parents are in their mid-eighties, and yet I see them traveling, reading history books, and watching documentaries on television. They never stop learning, and they talk about what they have learned with great enthusiasm.

6. Take the long-term view.

Think about your legacy, not the day-to-day. No matter what is happening now, what are you leaving the world? What has been your contribution? For me, that legacy is our children, despite the fact that my name is on the front cover of more than 100 books. No matter how hard I work, or how much I enjoy it, my most important lifetime achievement will always be the two children I gave birth to and my two stepchildren. Our four children (and their spouses and even their dogs) are what make me happy. I know that my face glows when someone asks about the kids... or their dogs. I'd rather talk about them than anything else.

7. And finally, take some time for yourself.

Sometimes, I don't get home from work till eight o'clock and I'm dead tired. But before I go into the house to start what I call the second shift, I'll sit in the car for an extra minute, listening to the end of an interesting news report or a song. Or I go for a walk and listen to an audiobook. That's "me" time. No matter how tired I am, or how late I go to bed, I take ten or fifteen minutes to read. That's "me" time, too. You've already given yourself the gift of some "me" time by reading this book. While you read the powerful stories in this book, you are recharging your batteries, gaining perspective on your current issues, and remembering what you're grateful for in your life.

One of the key lessons I learned from *Chicken Soup for the Soul: Find Your Happiness* was the value of purpose and passion. Even the most unhappy people can be transformed by seeing a purpose in their lives, or in pursuing a long buried passion.

One of my favorite people in the Chicken Soup for the Soul family is the exuberant, energetic Robin Pressnall. She is not only a wonderful writer and a funny and warm person, but she has also rescued more than 10,000 adorable, fluffy, little dogs. It is her life's passion and she gives, gives, and then gives more in her quest to save as many Bichon Frises as she can through her nonprofit Small Paws Rescue, the largest single-breed rescue organization in the U.S.

> *Even the most unhappy people can be transformed by seeing a purpose in their lives.*

It wasn't always that way for Robin, as she tells us in her story, "Filling a Need." Robin was approaching her fortieth birthday when she decided that something was missing from her life. She had friends and a loving husband, but with no children, she wondered what her legacy would be.

She was watching TV one day and saw Billy Graham speaking about prayer. He said that we should ask God for the "desires of our hearts." Robin's desire was to be someone who mattered. She says, "I wanted to make a difference in the lives of people and in the lives of animals… I thought that my 'purpose' would somehow include my love of singing, writing, travel, and of course, working with animals."

Then, one of Robin's dogs died after a long battle with cancer. Robin went to buy a Bichon Frise puppy—a new friend for her other dog—and encountered her first puppy mill. She says the place was "a nightmare."

Our heroine decided to delay her search for her "purpose" while she researched puppy mills and tried to stop the horrible one she had discovered in her own neighborhood. She formed her rescue organization and started sending out a newsletter to a couple of dozen people.

A few years passed and Robin's newsletter was being read by 6,000 people in twenty-eight countries. National media outlets began asking her to do interviews and to film episodes for Animal Planet. She still thought that she had temporarily put aside her search for "her purpose" while she helped the adorable, fluffy, little dogs.

It took Robin a while to realize that she had *already* found her purpose. She says, "I've been made whole and complete, and what more could any person ever ask? The sheer joy of doing what I do overflows from every pore of my body, and I can never repay this wonderful gift that has given my life purpose."

Every time I speak to Robin I am struck by her joy in her purposeful life, despite the tragedy she often sees in her rescue efforts. She knows that every morning she is embarking on another day during which she will make a difference. Finding her purpose and pursuing her passion was Robin's direct path to happiness.

***

Finding your purpose and passion is all well and good if you know what you want to do. But what if you have no idea? I'm going to share a couple of stories with you that may help you jump-start the process of finding your own happiness.

JC Sullivan describes one such very effective method in her story, "What If You Won the Lottery," in that same book, *Chicken Soup for the Soul: Find Your Happiness*. JC hated her job and one day she was complaining to her brother: "I have no idea what I want to do. I cannot stand banking."

Her brother had a great suggestion: "Imagine that you just won the lottery! What would be the first thing you'd do?"

Without even thinking, JC blurted out, "Oh my God! Move to Italy!" She had dreamed of living there since childhood.

"Then do it!" said her brother. "Move. I'm sick of hearing that you hate your job. I'll come visit."

JC pointed out that she had a ton of debt, but her brother didn't want to hear about it. He told her to start saving, do whatever it took to get out of debt, and focus on her goal — moving to Italy.

It was Henry Ford who said, "Obstacles are those frightful things you see when you take your eyes off your goal." JC focused on *her* goal. She threw all her energy into getting out of debt. She stopped carrying extra cash and put her credit cards in her freezer. She paid down her credit card debt and started practicing her Italian. She canceled absolutely everything that cost money. Nothing was as crucial as getting to Italy.

While JC was preparing to move, her work stress diminished merely from knowing that she would be leaving her job eventually. She also started playing mind games with herself — packing a suitcase and putting her passport inside it so she was ready to go. She says that every time she saw that passport inside the suitcase it made it real for her.

And then the day came, and JC was off to Milan. She says, "I didn't know what would happen in Italy, but one thing was for sure — even on its worst day, it had to be more interesting than my boring life as a stressed-out, debt-ridden banker."

JC says, "My imaginary lottery win forced me to listen to my inner voice and that imaginary lottery ticket turned into a real plane ticket. Deciding to move was a turning point in my life. My brother Sean knew that money had always been my obstacle. He simply removed money from the discussion and asked me to envision a different reality. Because so many of us use money as an excuse not to do something, I love this way of thinking and still use it when I'm trying to decide my next steps."

I love that story and when I was telling it on my podcast, I suddenly remembered something. When I traveled around Brazil as a college student, interviewing poets and singers, I would always ask them, "What would you do if you won the *loteria*?" It was a great way to get them talking to me honestly. They would get dreamy looks on their faces and they would always have an answer ready. Imagining what you would do if you won the lottery really does get you in touch with your true path to happiness. What a great way to figure out what you want!

***

There's another easy way to figure out what you want to do, and that is to make a bucket list of everything you want to do before you die, even if you are decades away from that fateful day. Life is about how you spend it, and my final story in this chapter is about that — what one woman learned when she was told she had one year to live.

Esther Griffin tells us what happened in "A Year to Live," which we published in *Chicken Soup for the Soul: From Lemons to Lemonade*. First of all, Esther was feeling just fine and was only in her mid-fifties, but she strained her back at work when she moved an old, heavy wooden desk. She was bedridden for days and then she finally hobbled to her car and went to the doctor for an X-ray.

The doctor reported that her back would heal by itself but the X-ray showed a spot on her kidney. When a CAT scan revealed a cancerous tumor, Esther had it removed. Unfortunately, it was a type of cancer that would not respond to treatment and the doctors said they couldn't determine whether they got it all, meaning she might only have one year to live. They told her to take a cruise and enjoy herself.

First Esther fought back. She wasn't even old enough to collect any of the money she had contributed to her Social Security account during all her years working for the school district. But then she decided that if she had only one year left she was going to make the most of it and finally focus on what she cared about.

She gave away most of her possessions and devoted herself to doing what was most meaningful to her. "If I had only a year, I was going to make it count," said Esther. "A plea for volunteers at our local zoo appeared in the newspaper. I signed up for the twenty-three-week course to learn all about animals and how to handle them.

"The newsletter for my genealogy society arrived, hand printed, with genealogy misspelled and a plea for a volunteer editor. I had only a year, but I could surely do better than that! So I became an editor."

Editing that newsletter made Esther realize that she could write, so she decided to use some of her last year to write and she sold a few pieces.

When the year ended and she was still around, Esther decided to take advantage of her reprieve. After all, how much more time might she have? So she did everything she had ever wanted to do: she took Spanish and Russian; she taught night school courses in genealogy and family history; and she spent as much time as she could with her young grandchildren, aware that she might not see them grow up.

> "Make yourself necessary to somebody."

Today that fifty-something woman is in her eighties. She has ten grandchildren and four great-grandchildren. She's been a zoo volunteer for more than twenty-five years. She is the editor of a local historical society newsletter and she's had several articles and a couple of children's books published.

Esther reports that she continues to live every year as if it's her last, a strategy that has been working very well for each and asker that sounds heavenly; you can get even more done! Nevertheless, I don't think I'm a proficient enough dreamer [to ass]ign myself problems to work on in my sleep. But in the [meant]ime, I can practice my dream analysis skills, or my dream [mean]ing," and at least pay attention to what my subconscious [has to] say while I'm asleep.

There's a great adage attributed to the Talmud, which says, "A [drea]m that is not interpreted is like a letter that is not read." I'm [going] to share some stories with you that support this advice and [dram]atically illustrate why it's so important to listen to our dreams.

***

[On]e of my most popular early podcasts was one in which I told [Dre]ma Sizemore Drudge's story, "Wake-Up Call." Drema, by the [wa]y, is pronounced "Dream-a," which is a fun fact in this context!

In her dream, Drema was walking into a funeral home to see [her] husband laid to rest. She smelled the overwhelming scent of [all] those different types of flowers mixed together, she saw that [gle]aming oak casket, and she bent down to say her final farewell [to] him.

And then, mercifully, Drema woke up, crying, and realized it [w]as just a dream. But when she looked over at her husband's side [o]f the bed he wasn't there. She was panic-stricken for a moment [a]nd then she realized he had gone in to work early that day. She [w]as still nervous though, so she called him at work to make sure [h]e was okay. And then, uncharacteristically, she said on the phone [t]o him, "I love you."

Drema explains that she and her husband had been going through a challenging time in their marriage when she had that dream. They had made an unsuccessful move to a new state for a job that failed to materialize. And even after they moved back home, and her husband found a good job again, Drema hadn't

every one of her twenty-five "last" years of life!

Albert Einstein said: "There are only two ways to live your life. One is as though nothing is a miracle. The other is as though everything is a miracle." Esther's approach sounds like a good way for all of us to live, one miraculous year after another.

***

Three stories; three different approaches to finding happiness. Each approach and result is eminently do-able.

That's because happiness is not a mysterious, elusive lottery ticket meant for only a lucky, random few. It is a jackpot within everyone's grasp once we remove the obstacles we put in our own paths and give ourselves permission to do the things we love to do.

After we've cleared the debris out of the road, our purpose, passion, and mission in life may be right there in front of us.

What You Can L
While You're As

Your dreams are a window i
what you already know

There's another way you can tap into
you happy, and that is to pay at
dreams. Dreams are a window into w
know about yourself. During the da
ing hours — you're distracted by tasks and people
noise, and it's hard to push those aside and get in to
innermost thoughts and desires. But at night, whe
in bed asleep, you're not distracted. That's when
scious can tell you all the things you *already* know al
but are too preoccupied to *hear* while you're awake.

One of the coolest things I get to do in my job is
about topics that I would like to know more about.
been fascinated by dreams and the things we learn abou
in our dreams, so last year I teamed up with one of t
most prominent dream experts, Kelly Sullivan Walde
coauthored *Chicken Soup for the Soul: Dreams and Prem*

The stories in this book convinced me that we know
better than we think, and we can access that subconscious k
of ourselves by paying attention to our dreams. The re
experts even know how to use their dreams *proactively* to
their lives. Kelly told me that she actually assigns hersel
to dream about before she goes to bed. What a great idea

multit
N
to ass
mean
"liste
has t

drea
goin
dran

On
Dre
wa

he
all
gl
to

w
o
a

recovered from the years of worrying about money. She knew she had a bad attitude but she didn't know how to change it.

She had tried prayer, self-help books, and talking to friends, all to no avail. So she had pushed the problem to the side, choosing to focus on her own life and ignore her husband. She went back to college, which was expensive, and she made a new set of friends, who she went out with nearly every weekend, leaving her husband out of her social life. Drema says she was acting like a teenager.

That was until she had that dream, which made her realize she'd been neglecting her husband and taking him for granted. He had been working overtime to pay for her college classes; he cooked on the nights she had to study for exams; and he drove her to some of those social events she had with her new friends.

> "A dream that is not interpreted is like a letter that is not read."

All of a sudden, Drema saw what she had been doing. She was deeply ashamed of her behavior. She says, "I owed this man so much more than an apology, and I quickly got busy." She cleaned the house thoroughly for the first time in a long time. She went shopping and bought a new dress that she thought he'd like. Then she got her hair done before buying the groceries to make him his favorite dinner of fried chicken, mashed potatoes, and green beans. She also stocked up on his favorite snacks, something else she hadn't bothered to do in a long time.

When her husband came home that night he found Drema dressed up and waiting for him at the front door, holding a blue envelope. The card inside contained a note apologizing for her behavior, for complaining and nagging, for focusing on the negative and downplaying the positive.

After he read the card, they both broke down in tears. That night they talked over dinner, the first real conversation they'd had in a long time. Drema assured him she wouldn't take him for granted again.

Drema won't forget the lesson of that nightmare. She says, "If I ever think I am beginning to take him for granted nowadays, I stop, close my eyes and think about that dream, that nightmare, and I imagine what would happen if it came true. It changes my attitude every time."

***

It's interesting that our dreams don't only give us direction, but also force us to confront the reality of our own behavior. This happened to Drema and it also happened to middle-school student Mariah Reyes, who shares her story, "From Bully to Best Friend."

Like many kids who were bullied, Mariah became a bully herself. She wrote, "I didn't know how to deal with my problems in a healthy way, so instead I took out all my sadness and anger on other people. I was verbally abusive, and at times I would say hurtful things to those around me without even considering how they might feel."

Mariah got two suspensions from school and lost many of her friends. Finally, in eighth grade, she had a dream in which she recognized what she had become. In the dream, she was walking around school listening to all the people she'd bullied talk about how she made them feel. It was like she was a ghost, moving among the other students invisibly while listening to them pour out their hurt.

"I'm sorry, I'm sorry, I'm sorry!" Mariah shouted in her dream, but no one could hear her. Mariah says that in her waking life, she wouldn't have cared, but the real Mariah, the compassionate girl she was supposed to be, was the Mariah in charge of her dream. That Mariah said, "I'm so sorry for all the pain I've caused you. Please forgive me." That Mariah was in tears.

When she woke up, she sobbed for twenty minutes, thinking, "I have to apologize for all of the horrible things I have said and done to those I bullied." The first thing she did was apologize to every person she could remember bullying. Almost everyone accepted her apology, and most of them forgave her.

Ever since that dream, Mariah has been a different person, or maybe I should say she has been her real self again. Her subconscious knew… and it was only through dreaming that Mariah could put aside the pressures of her waking life to reintroduce herself to the real person she was meant to be.

***

Mariah and Drema both became better versions of themselves as a result of their dreams, but we also read a lot of stories from people who learn something else from their dreams: they diagnose their own medical problems.

That's what Kristi Woods' dream did for her. She wrote a story called "Tested, Not Arrested" for our dreams book.

Kristi's dream started with her being pulled over by a burly Honolulu police officer, who then asked her to blow into a machine. Kristi was bright red with embarrassment. Why did the cop want her to take a Breathalyzer test? She hadn't been drinking and she was driving just fine.

She struggled to blow hard enough into the machine he handed her, but eventually she got it right. The police officer seemed pleased and took the device back to his patrol car. He leaned into it and pulled out a small, but thick, handheld machine that resembled a calculator. It looked like the ones delivery people use to obtain signatures.

The police officer consulted the machine and returned to Kristi's car, announcing, "You are most definitely lactose intolerant."

She was perplexed. Why was the police officer checking her for lactose intolerance? Then she woke up and realized it was a dream, but it got her thinking. She *had* been having digestive problems. Maybe she *was* lactose intolerant.

Kristi decided to stop consuming products made with milk. Sure enough, her abdominal symptoms disappeared. She never even went to a doctor. Problem solved. By listening to her dream.

How could this happen? Somehow Kristi knew she was lactose intolerant, but with all the distractions of daily life she had been ignoring what she subconsciously knew. Maybe she had heard people discussing lactose intolerance; maybe she had seen an advertisement for Lactaid. Whatever the reason, her subconscious had been gathering this information and processing it, but Kristi, in her waking life, had been ignoring it.

It's a great reminder to listen to your dreams. Because when you're asleep and all the noise of daily life disappears you can focus on what's essential. And you can learn about yourself — the stuff you actually already know but are too distracted to take in as you hustle through your days.

***

The dreams I've mentioned so far are not hard to analyze. They come right out and tell you what you need to know. But your subconscious might also provide you with a dream that takes a little more time to figure out. Linda Jackson had such a dream, which she relates in her story, "First Things First," in *Chicken Soup for the Soul: Dreams and Premonitions*.

Linda's daughters were in fifth grade and kindergarten when she had the dream that changed everything. She and her husband had just started a new ministry, and as part of that ministry, they volunteered at an afterschool program, Monday through Friday, from three o'clock until well into the evening, sometimes not arriving home until eight.

Then Linda was offered a paid job at the afterschool program, and she welcomed the extra income and responsibility. But that increased her hours even more. Her daughters would come to the program and hang out with the other kids, and her fifth grader would do her homework there. Sometimes they didn't get home until nine.

Things were going so well that Linda was offered the position of director of the whole program. This was a big promotion, and an opportunity to have a bigger positive impact on all the kids. But the hours would get even worse. Linda was feeling guilty. She was giving so much of her time to the other children and not enough to her own.

Linda decided to think about the director position for a while. And then she had a dream about her neighbor's yard. Her neighbor's yard had always been lovely, well maintained. But in the dream, the once well-cared-for lawn was overgrown with weeds. Her neighbor, looking haggard and worn, told her, "I've been so busy taking care of other people's yards, that I haven't had time to take care of my own."

Linda woke up and thought, "Wow, I can't believe how horrible Mr. Jones's yard looked." And then she dismissed the dream and went on with her day.

Later that morning, she randomly opened the Bible to Song of Solomon, and read: "My mother's children were angry with me; they made me the keeper of the vineyards; but mine own vineyard have I not kept."

This is starting to get obvious to us now that we know the power of dreams. Linda saw the connection, but not enough to do anything about it.

Then, Linda's older daughter started having trouble with her grades. And Linda realized that her family barely had time to gobble down dinner before going to bed.

That's when Linda finally heeded the dream. She quit working at the afterschool program, and she tended to her own "vineyard." Better late than never, right?

***

There's another kind of dream that we all have, those recurring ones: the didn't-study-for-the-exam dream, the out-in-public-naked dream, the flying dream, the falling dream, and the looking-desperately-for-the-restroom dream. Another common recurring dream is one I have had many times, in which I wander down a hallway in my house and discover a whole wing I have never noticed before, complete with two empty bedrooms and a bathroom. I am delighted to have found this extra space!

> Dreams are a window into what you already know about yourself.

I examine every detail of these newly discovered rooms, which are unusual in their design, with multiple levels. They will be lots of fun to decorate and use. Then I wake up and realize it was a dream. I am always disappointed.

I mentioned this recurring dream to my brother Andrew and he said he has the same dream all the time, too. And when I surveyed my co-workers at Chicken Soup for the Soul, almost everyone reported having the same dream, usually involving the discovery of an extra wing in their houses.

The psychologist Erick Fromm said, "A dream is a microscope through which we look at the hidden occurrences in our soul." More like hidden spaces in this case, right? Why do we have this deep-seated need to find more space in our homes? I always thought it was just me, so I'm fascinated by the fact that almost everyone in our office reports the same thing.

There's a website called The Dream Well (thedreamwell.com) where I found an article by Amy Campion in which she reports that this common dream can be frightening for some people. She says that our reaction to finding one or more new rooms in our dreams can give us some insight into ourselves. Some people view these new rooms as a challenge or an obligation they don't want. Others are excited about the opportunity to expand their lives. And some people find the rooms fully furnished, while others find them empty, filled with possibility but also needing a lot of work! According to Amy Campion, "Dreams of new rooms can be exciting dreams of emerging new potential and the promise of growth and experience."

I'm glad that almost everyone in my office reports they are excited when they find the new rooms and disappointed when they wake up and realize it's not true. I guess we're an adventurous lot, willing to take on new challenges. It certainly makes sense, since we put out a new Chicken Soup for the Soul book every month, and we are a busy and creative group of people. I sure hope that our common dream really does mean we're up for any challenge.

Or maybe I'm overanalyzing and all it means is that I want more space! After all, we have four grown kids, two already married and one getting married next year, and we've already cleaned and organized the old toys and created a playroom area for the theoretical grandchildren. It could be as simple as that.

But more often than not, the images, stories, feelings, and words in our dreams can mean something deeper than what they show on the surface. My high school English teacher, Mr. Davis, would send me out of class for saying this, but no other word will do: Our dreams can be illuminating and *symbolic* of our fears, hopes and issues — past, present, and future. Paying attention to our dreams is like looking in the mirror. We get to really see ourselves.

My Mother Is an Alien

Dare to be different
when raising children

"**M**ommy, what are we?" asked my seven-year-old son. We were sitting at the kitchen table with his five-year-old sister and my first husband. I knew why Mike was asking; he had heard his friends talking about their parents' religions and diverse backgrounds.

This was 100% unplanned and I don't know what came over me, but I assumed a serious demeanor and said, "Mike, I think you and Ella are old enough to know the truth." It sounded like I was about to tell them they were adopted. My husband had no idea what I was doing, but he stayed silent as I continued.

"Your father is Catholic… and I am an alien. So you are half Catholic and half alien." The kids' mouths were hanging open. Mike later told me that he had been hoping they were adopted so that he wouldn't have the same genes as his annoying little sister.

I continued to improvise: "In alien families, there is a marker person in each generation so that all the aliens will be able to recognize each other. My father's name is Allan, and that name is spelled almost like 'alien.' In my generation, I am the marker since my initials are ALN and if you say A-L-N really fast it sounds like 'alien.' Ella, your middle name is Anne. If you say 'Ella Anne' really fast, what does it sound like? It sounds like 'alien.'"

By then, the children had caught on to the fact that I was kidding, but I had started a wonderful new family tradition with the kids. I ordered a vanity plate from the Connecticut DMV and everyone at school knew that Mike and Ella's mom drove the "AlienMobile" with the ALIEN license plate.

I definitely raised my children in an unconventional manner, but it was because I tried to put myself *in their shoes*. Adults are always telling children what to do, even when it's not necessary. My parenting philosophy was to give my kids a lot of responsibility in areas where it wasn't critical that they get it right, so that they could have *some* say over their lives and feel in control of at least *some* decisions.

The first big test of this occurred shortly after their father and I got divorced, and it involved gerbils — lots of them. Remember my big mouth? Well, the day that we announced the divorce to the kids, I blurted out that I would provide them with the following "perks": bunk beds, a trip to Disney World, and pet gerbils.

After we moved into my new house, I took Mike and Ella to the pet store for the promised baby gerbils. The salesperson turned the pups over, checked their equipment, and assured us they were both girls.

It wasn't long before we discovered that our babies had made two more babies. Poor Taz just hadn't been that well endowed as a kid, and Speedy, the female, had lived up to her name.

At this point, I was supposed to return one of the gerbils to the pet store, which had a money-back policy if a same sex couple proved to be not so *same* after all. But we couldn't give up

Taz *or* Speedy, so instead, I arranged for Taz to have a vasectomy performed by a microsurgeon.

I was going to buy a $500 vasectomy for a $7 gerbil. Because that's what mothers do.

The day of the vasectomy, I found myself sitting with my legs tightly crossed, and I realized I couldn't go through with it. So I called off the surgery and, to celebrate, those gerbils had another litter and this time there were six little rascals to outplace.

This was getting out of hand, so I separated Taz and Speedy for several months. But Speedy had another litter anyway, some kind of immaculate conception according to the other residents of my house, who denied arranging any conjugal visits.

Ella is an OB/GYN now so she remains the lead suspect, especially since the gerbils were both housed in her room in their separate cages. This may have been her first effort to aid a couple in conceiving a child.

After the surprise litter, I gave in and officially put the happy pair back together. After all, Taz had to help with the babies. It was the responsible thing to do. Thus began what I call The Breeding Years and what Bill, by then in the process of becoming my second husband, calls The Something-Smells-Really-Bad Years.

Even though she was only eight, Ella promised to do all the work. As a newly single mother, it seemed like a good experiment to me. If she could handle that kind of responsibility, I was all for it.

Ella came through with flying colors. She cleaned the cage, fed the gerbils, kept them active and healthy, and even buried the occasional dead body.

Most important, she helped find homes for all of the baby gerbils. We became proficient at palming off those babies on other families. Every time we had a litter, Ella would take the babies to school for Show and Tell. When a mother would call and unenthusiastically say, "My kid wants one of those baby gerbils," I would explain that gerbils were social creatures and had to be adopted in pairs. Ella was very good at figuring out which ones were girls and which ones were boys, much better than the guy at the pet store, so that we could outplace the babies in matched pairs.

Over three years, those healthy, well-cared-for gerbils had sixty-two babies and Ella found homes for all of them.

And then, sadly, a week after she delivered a new litter, Speedy died.

The autopsy showed that she was full of tumors, not uncommon for an elderly gerbil.

Yes, I paid for an autopsy on the gerbil.

***

Ella rose to the challenge when it came to caring for those gerbils, which proved to me that kids can handle a lot more responsibility than adults think.

The nineteenth-century humorist and writer, Henry Wheeler Shaw, who used the pen name Josh Billings, had some good advice about childrearing: "To bring up a child in the way he should go, travel that way yourself once in a while." In other words, imagine what it feels like to have no say over your life, even for little decisions like whether you get to stay up an hour past your usual bedtime. It can be pretty frustrating!

> *I had always found that my kids behaved better if I gave them some control over the unimportant things.*

There had to be a better way. We needed to coexist with me in charge, but with the kids feeling like it was not a total dictatorship. So I decided to make it a *benevolent* dictatorship.

The kids always behaved better when I gave them control over the unimportant things, such as how they styled their hair or what clothes they wore. Mike wore a red cape to nursery school for an entire semester because that made him happy, and Ella insisted on wearing Mike's outgrown khaki pants to school for a year. They looked awful on her, but it wasn't worth a battle.

I figured that if I let the kids make those kinds of decisions, they wouldn't feel the need to rebel about the things that mattered, such as doing their best in school or avoiding self-destructive behavior.

This led to one of my best gift ideas ever! One Christmas, when they were preteens, I surprised the kids with homemade coupon books. I took their most requested privileges, made coupons for them, and stapled them into a little booklet that included:

1 coupon for "Shopping spree at the mall"
2 coupons for "A day with Mom doing anything you want"
2 coupons for "Have a party for whatever reason you want"
4 coupons for "Pick a game to play with Mom"
4 coupons for "Double your allowance this week"
4 coupons for "Triple your allowance this week"
4 coupons for "Get candy while shopping with Mom"
5 coupons for "Order pizza whenever you want"
12 coupons for "Have one can of soda whenever you want"
12 coupons for "Stay up one hour past bedtime"
12 coupons for "Watch one hour of TV on a school night"
12 coupons for "Watch one hour of TV on a camp night"

In the early years, I also included coupons like "Have Mom read a book to you" and in the later years I included things like "Get a ride for you and your friends to the movies."

The kids loved their booklets. They presented me with a coupon whenever they wanted to exercise one of their privileges. They had power, we had peace, and we could spend more time enjoying each other instead of negotiating. They learned how to budget their TV time; they chose when it was really important to stay up late; and they learned to view candy and soda as occasional treats over which they had control. After all, they had to make those coupons last an entire year until the next Christmas.

I continued to give them their privilege coupons through their middle school years. I think it was one more contribution to making them the responsible adults they are today. They still talk about those coupons and how much they liked them, and I won't be surprised if my grandchildren end up getting privilege coupons from their parents, too!

> *"If you want children to keep their feet on the ground, put some responsibility on their shoulders."*

I used the same philosophy when it came to the kids' clothing—giving them more responsibility for their decisions at an early age. I had gotten the idea when we were at Disney World. I loved going to Disney World with the kids, but there was one downside. Souvenirs. The kids would drive me nuts asking for souvenirs, to the point that in the stores I would try to block Ella's view of the stuffed animals and Mike's view of the superhero items.

Then I discovered Disney Dollars, paper currency with Mickey Mouse printed on the bills! The next time we went to Disney World, I bought each child fifty Disney Dollars to spend on souvenirs. They started evaluating every possible purchase as if they worked for Consumer Reports, and they returned home with half their Disney Dollars unspent.

That gave me an idea when I was at my wit's end over Mike's remarkable ability to lose his clothes. Their school had a dress code and it could get expensive. I'll never forget when twelve-year-old Mike went off to the first day of school in a brand-new, navy blue blazer and came home wearing a bedraggled old one that barely fit him. The $100 blazer that I had bought just a little too big for him, so that it would last the entire school year, was gone. He said his friend Gideon needed a larger jacket so they swapped.

That was the last straw in a series of clothing disappearances.

I decided it was time to change the dynamic in our household. I sat the kids down and laid out their annual clothing budget. Their father and I would give them half their budget in the fall and half in the spring.

That changed everything. I drove them to the stores, we shopped together, and we each paid for our own purchases. If Mike lost something, it was not my problem, and he learned a lesson about caring for his possessions. There were no arguments over clothing, no pleading for more, and no frustration on either side. We actually had fun shopping together.

I know that giving children their own budgets at ages ten and twelve was unusual, but it worked for us. The advice columnist Abigail Van Buren summed it up perfectly when she said, "If you want children to keep their feet on the ground, put some responsibility on their shoulders." I gave my children the responsibility for what they wore on their shoulders, literally! Mike became much more careful, although he did lose his blazer one more time, the night before an important ninth-grade event. With my new attitude, I thought it was funny when he had to wear a pastel plaid jacket from the Lost and Found.

***

It might have looked like I was a permissive parent, but in fact I was raising kids who learned early to budget their money, value their privileges, and accept responsibility for their decisions. And again, because I focused on winning the big battles and not the unimportant skirmishes, I let them make their own decisions on the state of their rooms.

The rule was that they couldn't leave one smidgeon of mess in the rest of the house, not even in the family room, but their bedrooms were their domains.

This led to some fancy footwork on my part. When they called from school or from their father's house, asking me to please find a missing something or other in their rooms, I had to tiptoe my way across a floor covered with papers, duffel bags, sports apparel, receipts, and more—all the detritus of preteen and teenage life. I allowed this mess for three reasons: 1) because I remembered my own very messy teen years; 2) because they had to live in two houses — mine and their father's; and 3) because I was too busy to bother with a trivial thing like a messy bedroom that wasn't hurting anyone except its occupant. When I had people over, I just closed the kids' bedroom doors.

The funny thing was that once the kids went off to college and had their "own places," they got a lot neater. It was lurking inside them all along!

***

So how did these children turn out? Pretty well, I think. They were kind enough to go to the same college, Georgetown, and graduate on the same day. Mike took a gap year before he went, living in Spain and becoming fluent in Spanish, and Ella hurried up and graduated in three years. So this very busy mom only had to attend one college graduation! When people hear that my kids graduated from the same college on the same day, they ask if they are twins. I always say, "They are now, but they used to be two years apart."

Mike is twenty-nine now, and an author and journalist. He is married to Emily, who is getting her Ph.D. in neuroscience at Boston University.

Ella is twenty-seven, and after getting her medical degree at Brown, she is a resident at Dartmouth in New Hampshire, where her fiancé, Josh, is getting his Ph.D. in engineering. You can see the whole gang in this photo taken at her med school graduation: Mike and Emily, Bill, me, Ella and Josh, Tim, and Rosey and Joey.

The kids get along handsomely with their new sister and brother, my stepchildren Rosey and Tim. Bill and I did something that worked well for us when we got married and blended the two pairs of kids. We took a long vacation with them every year, visiting offbeat places such as the Galapagos Islands, Peru, Bolivia, the Baltic Sea, and Australia. We also skied together in the winter near where Tim and Rosey went to college. These shared experiences created a strong bond between the four kids and they have gotten along beautifully from day one of our marriage.

Tim is creating a lot of excitement in our family now, as he has recently written and directed a full-length film that we all expect to do very well. At age thirty-seven, after spending more than a decade in the film industry as an actor, writer, director, and producer, I'm pretty sure he is going to be an "overnight success." The only thing wrong with Tim is that he lives in LA.

Rosey is thirty-four and a mental health counselor specializing in children and teens. Her husband Joey is a musician and high-end audio expert. Rosey is the "good child" because she and Joey live the closest to us, in the Hudson Valley of New York.

Maybe that is the only thing that we did wrong as parents... we raised these independent children who live too far away. The author Elizabeth Stone is famous for having said, "Making the decision to have a child is momentous. It is to decide forever to have your heart go walking around outside your body." There are definitely little pieces of my heart in four different places.

Why You Should Listen to Your Mother... Forever

Mom and Dad can come to your rescue even after they're gone

may be an alien, but I still believe I know what is best for my kids. Most mothers do. And now that Mike and Ella are in their late twenties, I find they are willing to listen to my ideas and advice more and more. So you can imagine how much I enjoy all the stories we get at Chicken Soup for the Soul about grown kids who are still listening to their moms... even after their mothers have passed away.

No matter what your belief system, it's hard to explain away most of these stories. Sometimes the power of a parent's love and the bond with a child can be so strong that it seems to transcend death. In the past few years, we've published dozens of fascinating, mindboggling stories about parents who seem to reach out from beyond the grave to help their children — when they are sick or in danger or need to solve a complicated problem.

One way of looking at this phenomenon is to say that your subconscious can talk to you in your parents' voices, telling you what you already know they would have said. After all those years of listening to their advice, you may already have a good idea of what they would tell you.

Another way to view it is that they are truly sending messages from some spiritual place beyond this world. Many of our writers are certain their parents are sending messages from heaven, and they report that there is "no way" that they could have subconsciously known what their parents are now telling them.

However it happens, one thing is for sure: the children who hear from their parents are left in awe and grateful for the connection. And I get shivers from these stories and love passing them on to you, because the one thing I *do* know is that there's a lot of stuff we *don't* know!

The stories I'm going to tell you next are so incredible, they have stuck with me over the years and they prove the old adage that truth is stranger than fiction.

***

Here's a great example of a mindboggling story that is hard to explain. It has an excellent title that every mother believes — "Mom Knows Best" — and we published it in *Chicken Soup for the Soul: Messages from Heaven*. The story opens with Carolyn Hall in terrible pain following abdominal surgery. Her doctor said this was normal, but it was already *ten days* post-surgery.

It was the middle of the night so Carolyn went downstairs to the living room so she wouldn't wake up her husband, John. She collapsed into the recliner and then something weird happened. She felt like an invisible force was pressing her to the chair — she couldn't move. She couldn't call out to her husband for help either; she tried, but no sound came out.

Carolyn was pretty frightened until she felt a sudden flood of warmth and love. Somehow she knew it was her mom, who had died eight years earlier.

And then Carolyn sensed her mom giving her a message: "Tell Dr. Hughes you've got blood clots."

John found Carolyn in the morning, still glued to the recliner and white as a ghost. She explained that she needed to speak to the doctor but she couldn't move. John wanted to call an ambulance to get her to the hospital but Carolyn insisted: Her mom had specifically told her to tell the doctor.

As it turned out, Dr. Hughes was in surgery and Carolyn couldn't see him until the early afternoon. When she finally did, he proclaimed that Carolyn had pneumonia. He reprimanded her for being too inactive after her surgery, saying she had brought on the pneumonia. Carolyn said no, explaining, "I haven't been in bed. We've got a two-story house and my office is in the basement. I've been working part-time since my first day home."

> *Sometimes the power of a parent's love and the bond with a child can be so strong that it seems to transcend death.*

"That may be true, but you still have pneumonia," said the doctor. "I'll order an X-ray to be sure, but we'll send you home with antibiotics. You'll be good as new in a few days."

He called for a chest X-ray and showed Carolyn: "Yep, pneumonia."

Carolyn insisted. "I don't have pneumonia. I have blood clots."

"Are you a doctor?"

"No. My mom told me to tell you I have blood clots."

"Is she a doctor?"

"No. She's been dead for eight years."

Somehow that worked. Dr. Hughes got on the phone and called someone: "I've got someone I need you to see. Her X-ray shows pneumonia. She's ten days post-op from abdominal surgery. But she's sure it's blood clots. I think we need to consider it."

Carolyn went for another test and sure enough she had three blood clots in her lungs. She was put in the ICU for a week and there a nurse told her that she had what were called "silent blood clots," ones that looked like pneumonia on a chest X-ray. She would need to stay glued to her bed so as not to dislodge those clots.

"They're easily overlooked and fatal," said the nurse. "You've got a sharp doctor to catch these. He saved your life."

The next morning, Dr. Hughes stopped by. "Just passing through but I wanted to know if your mom had anything else she thought I should know about."

***

Another story that lingers with me was published in *Chicken Soup for the Soul: Miraculous Messages from Heaven*. It's called "Conversations with Dad," and it's from Jackson Jarvis, who is the son of one of our executives, Joelle Jarvis.

This event happened when Jackson was only two and a half years old. His father had just died in a car accident. Jackson didn't understand the concept of death — he thought his dad was away on a business trip and would still be coming home.

One day, about a week after his dad died, Jackson was taking a bath and Joelle heard him having a conversation with someone. Jackson told her that he was talking to his dad and that his dad told him that he asked his friend Kirk, who had been his boss, to take Jackson horseback riding.

Joelle didn't pay much attention to this fantasy — Jackson had never gone horseback riding with Kirk before so it was just a little boy's imagination. It *was* strange that he mentioned Kirk, though, since he didn't really know him.

A few weeks later, after the post-funeral hubbub had died down and the Jarvis household was quiet again, there was a knock on the front door. Joelle opened it to find her husband's friend Kirk standing in the driveway holding the reins of a tall, dark brown horse. Jackson came out to see the horse and Kirk shook his hand and offered him a ride.

Then Kirk told Joelle what had happened. "Joelle, it was the weirdest thing — I was outside, standing in my front yard, and I swear I heard Eric's voice asking me to stop by and take Jackson horseback riding."

Jackson is a high school senior now. He says that from that day on, he always felt like his dad was watching out for him.

***

Another father-son connection story that is also astonishing comes to us from *Chicken Soup for the Soul: Dreams and Premonitions*. The story is called "Service Call" and it's by one of our regular writers, Connie Kaseweter Pullen.

Connie's husband had passed away a few years earlier and their son Chris had taken over the duties on the family's Christmas tree farm. There were five Pullen children but Chris was the one who had always loved working outdoors with his father, especially on the heavy equipment. Following in his father's footsteps seemed to help Chris ease the pain of his dad's untimely death.

The story opens with Chris trying to replace the clutch in his dad's old bulldozer. It had broken down right before he finished clearing out some overgrown trees from their land. Chris had only seen his dad replace the clutch once, when he was a little kid.

After spending hours puzzling over how to fix the bulldozer, Chris had dinner with his mom and went off to bed.

The next morning, Chris ran down the stairs and flew past Connie as she was standing at the stove frying some bacon and eggs. "Hey, what's the hurry?" she asked. "No time for breakfast?" He said he'd be back in a minute and ran out the back door to the bulldozer. Connie figured that he had come up with a new approach to fix the clutch.

She ate breakfast, cleaned up, and then went out to feed the chickens and gather eggs. She called out to Chris to see how he was doing. He poked his head out from under the bulldozer and shouted that things were going much better.

About an hour later, Chris came in the back door. Connie

went down to the kitchen and found him pouring himself a cup of black coffee.

He looked happy! "So, why the happy smile?" asked Connie. "And why were you in such a hurry to get out back this morning?"

"I had to see if Dad was right!" explained Chris.

Connie was perplexed. "I have no idea what you're talking about."

"I saw Dad last night!" said Chris. And he told the story: "Sometime during the night, I woke up and opened my eyes to see Dad lying on the couch in my bedroom. He was wearing his old blue and white plaid shirt, and his red Mack baseball cap was pulled down over his forehead.

> *"Death ends a life, not a relationship."*

"Dad just started talking as though nothing was unusual! He said, 'Chris, there's a hard-to-find bolt under the transmission that you have to remove in order to slide it out of the way.' He explained the entire repair job to me step by step in a way that made it perfectly easy for me to understand. I would never have figured it out if it hadn't been for his detailed instructions!"

Connie asked, "Did you have to tell him you were having a problem fixing the dozer?"

"No, he seemed to already know," said Chris. "Actually, I didn't say anything. Dad did all the talking."

Connie asked if he thought his dad was really there.

And Chris said, "I've never believed in seeing spirits or ghosts, but I know for a fact that I was awake! I also know that there is no way in the world that I would have had the knowledge to fix the dozer if Dad hadn't really been there! That bolt was so well hidden I would never have found it. But, I'm at a loss to explain what actually happened."

Connie says that neither she nor Chris knows how to explain it, except to say that Chris hadn't known there was a hidden bolt.

All that Connie can say is that she has faith that if Chris needed help, there is nothing his dad wouldn't have done to make sure he got it.

* * *

I could fill a book with stories like these. Oh yeah, I have! Here's another astounding one for you about a mother-daughter connection. It was written for *Chicken Soup for the Soul: Messages from Heaven*, and it's called "Love You Forever." We actually published it for a second time in a book that benefits the Boys & Girls Clubs of America: *Chicken Soup for the Soul: For Mom, with Love.*

Our wonderful writer Amy Chesler, who writes as A.B. Chesler, shares an event that occurred soon after her mother's murder by Amy's own troubled brother. Amy's mom was a beloved math teacher, known for going out of her way to help her students and friends. It was a tragic and senseless loss.

Amy made it through the funeral, even writing her mother's eulogy, which she tucked into her mom's favorite children's book, *Love You Forever*. Then she placed the book in her mother's arms.

After the funeral and all the other related events were over, Amy broke down. She still needed her mother and couldn't believe that she was gone. She would experience marriage, children — all those major life events — without her mother. Amy wished fervently for a sign that her mother was still watching over her.

Weeks passed and Amy was still a basket case. Finally her best friend forced her to leave the house — they would make a quick trip to Target just to get out and do something.

Once they were there, Amy was not into it. She didn't want anything, but her friend persuaded her to at least get some candy as a little pick-me-up. Amy picked something out and got in the checkout line. As she stood there waiting she looked up at the rack of impulse items, and on the very top, above the candy, hair ties, and hand sanitizer, sat a copy of *Love You Forever*, that children's book she had buried with her mother. She immediately felt her eyes well with tears.

Amy asked the cashier why the book was sitting on top of the candy display. There were no other books there. The cashier said that maybe someone had left it after changing his or her mind about buying it.

For some odd reason, Amy felt a strong urge to ask her where the rest of the copies of the book were in the store. The cashier tried to scan the book, but couldn't — the machine made a loud beeping noise.

"I'm sorry, ma'am," the cashier said to Amy. "This book isn't scanning because we have no other copies in-store. In fact, we haven't for a while. It says the last time we had this book in stock was two and a half years ago. I'm not really sure why it was sitting there... If you'd like to buy it ma'am, I apologize because I guess it's not really available for purchase. But... I mean... I guess you can... Just take it? It's not really ours to sell."

Amy cradled the book in her arms, and suddenly things looked better. It was the sign she was looking for.

I have to tell you a little more about Amy, because she gave us another story about her strong mother-daughter connection that we published in *Chicken Soup for the Soul: Hope & Miracles*. That story, "Let's Make a Deal," is about a cool coincidence that happened five years later. Amy was still missing her mom, of course. That will never stop. And she was trying to find her in their old family movies. But her mom was never in front of the camera, as she was always the one doing the filming. Then Amy realized that YouTube might have a video of her mom, who had been chosen from the audience to compete on *Let's Make a Deal* in the early 1970s.

She searched the Internet but didn't find a clip of her mother. But then she got a pop-up ad for *Let's Make a Deal* tickets. Amy filled out the form and asked for two tickets, and a few hours later she got an e-mail with tickets for the very next day! Amy and her husband quickly figured out their costumes and the next day, dressed as a pirate, Amy found herself standing in line, then sitting in the audience screaming, and then, miraculously, picked to compete!

What a coincidence! From the hundreds of guests in the audience, her mom had been chosen decades ago, and now Amy was chosen, too.

The other guest who was chosen with Amy lost everything when she picked the wrong door. She went back to her seat, leaving Amy to take a chance. She told the host Wayne Brady that her mother had been on the show forty years earlier, said that she knew her mom was watching over her, and then, with tears in her eyes, chose door number two.

And won a car!

***

When we lose someone, it is comforting to think that somehow we can remain in touch. The actor Jack Lemmon is quoted saying, "Death ends a life, not a relationship."

We may not be able to explain how Carolyn knew she had blood clots, how Chris learned how to fix the bulldozer, how little Jackson got his ride on the horse, or how that favorite book of Amy's mother appeared at the checkout counter, but it does open our eyes to the fact that there are some things we just can't be sure about.

Except, of course, that we should listen to our mothers.

Why I Would Be the World's Worst Therapist

Reading 20,000+ soulful stories puts life's challenges in perspective

have always said that I would be the world's worst therapist. If someone visited me in my office, snuggled into the couch, grabbed a box of Kleenex, and prepared for a good long pity party, he or she might be disappointed. It's because I've been exposed to so many Chicken Soup for the Soul stories that I've seen it all, and no matter what the problem, I would remind my new client that a million other people were having the same problem right then and there.

I'd have *some* compassion, of course, because we all need to express our hurt and anger and worry, but I wouldn't let my clients spend much time wallowing in their pain. Before their first sessions were over, I'd probably be saying, "Buck up. Get over yourself. It's not all about you. Lots of other people have successfully weathered this problem." And they'd either be instantly cured or hate me and never come back. Either way I'd be out of a job.

Besides the 20,000+ stories in our library that have become part of my personal experience, I've read many thousands more that were sent to us but not used. In the early years I would read every one of the thousands of stories that were submitted for each title. Now I have a whole team of editors who do that, and after consulting with me along the way about what they are finding, they narrow down the list to about 300 finalists for me to consider as we select the final 101 that will constitute each volume.

That's a lot of "case studies." And they have made me feel more like a psychologist than a publisher. I don't know the clinical names for everything, but I do know the feelings. I feel for our writers and I cry with them, laugh with them, and rejoice with them. We are often the first confidantes for them, and they share unbelievably personal stories with us, some so personal that we *can't* publish them. But they all contribute to what I feel has become my own better understanding of what makes people tick.

> "I freely admit that I am a Pollyanna. I look for rainbows after the storm."

Just by virtue of being the publisher and editor-in-chief of the *Chicken Soup for the Soul* series, I am exposed to stories outside the office, too. When I meet someone and my profession comes up, he or she often starts talking, and talking, and talking. I hear a lot. And I'm surprised by how readily the advice comes out of my mouth. I draw on all the personal experiences that have been shared with us and I recognize situations and can reliably predict possible outcomes and suggest solutions.

I think I've become a better mother, wife, daughter, sister, and friend as a result of this job. I'm more grounded, less judgmental, more compassionate, and just plain more knowledgeable about the human condition. Everyone says that I'm "so nice" now. What was I *before*? This question has not been asked or answered!

But I'm not nice enough to put up with narcissists. We don't include their stories in our books because we don't think that they are helpful, and because we have so many stories available from people who are positive role models. These people demonstrate resilience and inner strength. They overcome huge challenges. They actively look for the silver linings and find them.

I get to meet thousands of these inspirational people through their stories. And occasionally I even get to meet them in person. Last summer, I traveled around Colorado for a week holding four different "contributor events" at which we got to spend some time with almost one hundred of our writers. One of them was Cindy Charlton, who has stories published in our books about *Angels Among Us*, *Family Caregivers*, *From Lemons to Lemonade*, and *The Power of Positive*. You can see happy, positive Cindy smiling broadly in this photo of the whole group at our luncheon in Denver. Bill, D'ette, and I are over on the far left of the photo and Cindy is sitting in front of Bill, wearing the white pearls. The index cards everyone's holding up, by the way, show the number of stories each writer has in our books.

Cindy never fails to inspire me with her positive outlook. In her story "No Food for Alligators," she says, "I freely admit that I am a Pollyanna. I look for rainbows after the storm." Cindy has been accused of being "annoyingly happy." Her disposition is remarkable when you consider what she's been through.

Back when Cindy was a young mother, she woke up one morning feeling fine and by the evening was fighting for her life. She had contracted one of those horrible infections — Strep A necrotizing fasciitis — a "flesh-eating disease." The only way to stop those infections when they get out of control is to amputate the affected areas before the disease spreads even further. Cindy lost her right hand, the lower halves of both legs and the left side of her chest.

After the amputations she lay in her hospital bed, wondering how she was going to manage two small children, a husband, a home, and her job. But, during the months of treatment that followed, she managed to focus on the fact that she'd survived, and on what she still *had* instead of what she'd lost. Eventually she left the hospital feeling as if she'd been reborn.

> *As long as my kids are okay and I don't have a terminal disease, my problems are pretty minimal.*

Cindy adapted to the new version of her life — one that included prostheses and endless physical therapy. She cared for her two sons and helped them heal from the trauma of almost losing her. And she never lost her sense of humor. One morning she broke a prosthesis getting into her car. After dropping her son off at school, she told a friend she needed help. "I broke my foot," Cindy said. Her friend was horrified, momentarily forgetting that Cindy's foot was not made of flesh and blood. Then Cindy gestured toward the broken fake limb in the passenger seat next to her and they both laughed hysterically.

The story is even more remarkable because, just as Cindy was coming to terms with life as a triple amputee, tragedy struck her family again. Only two years after her husband acted as her caregiver and sole parent to their two children, he was diagnosed with terminal cancer and *she* became *his* caregiver. Of course, being Cindy, she has this positive thing to say about that: "Being the caregiver is invaluable, life-altering, and transcending. It is one of the most amazing gifts of all."

Cindy ultimately had to deal with the fallout from her triple amputation and her husband's death and keep her two young sons happy and healthy and not too overwhelmed by all that had befallen their family.

This woman is astonishing. She does a lot of motivational workshops and public speaking now and she calls herself the Disability Diva. Cindy sums up her positive attitude by saying, "If I only looked at what I've lost, I'd never be able to see what I have."

Cindy Charlton has certainly demonstrated the tremendous inner strength that a human being can have. And when we are feeling overwhelmed here at the office, invariably one of our editors will point to Cindy as a shining example of why we shouldn't feel sorry for ourselves.

I'm not saying that we don't all have the right to complain about our bad days or bad months or bad years. But my feeling is that as long as my kids are okay and I don't have a terminal disease, my problems are pretty minimal. And whatever problems I have are shared by millions of other people!

Small problems count. I'm not saying they don't. In the last couple of weeks, my boiler overflowed, my pool heater broke and had to be replaced at great expense (I know that's a "one percenter" problem), the air conditioning system iced up in our basement and had to be fixed, and I finished writing this book while recovering from surgery — to fix the damage from the thyroid eye disease that I mentioned in Chapter 3.

These problems — even the eye surgery — don't seem like much of anything to me after reading all the stories in our books. And if I do have a day when I'm feeling overwhelmed by my little problems, I give myself a shake and tell myself the same thing I might say to someone who stepped into my "therapy" office — *get over yourself, Amy!*

And then I count myself incredibly lucky.

CHAPTER
—15—

Count Your Blessings

Practicing gratitude makes you
happier and healthier

We didn't know that the greatest recession since the Great Depression was starting when we bought Chicken Soup for the Soul in April 2008, but I'm not complaining (as per the previous chapter). Plenty of people had it worse than us.

As we weathered the recession, which hit the publishing industry particularly hard, forcing Borders into bankruptcy and shuttering hundreds of independent bookstores, we also continued to provide support to our readers. In late 2008, our distributor, Simon & Schuster, asked us if we could make a book specifically about the recession and get it done *fast*. We rose to the challenge and only six months later we published *Chicken Soup for the Soul: Tough Times, Tough People*, in which half of the stories were specifically recession-related.

It was fascinating and inspiring for me, still new to the Chicken Soup for the Soul world, to see the tremendous spirit and resilience of our writers. Many stressed how happy they were despite lower incomes, smaller homes, and simpler lifestyles. The ones who weren't writing about the recession wrote about the new lives they had come to accept and enjoy after chronic illness, accidents, losing loved ones, or other non-economic challenges. Some were victims of a crime, some watched their houses burn down, and some were living with incurable illnesses or disabilities.

Many wrote about finding inner strength they didn't know they had. They wrote about tremendous support from their friends, or about their marriages strengthening in the face of adversity. There were lots of stories about families rediscovering the joy of spending time together — in their new smaller digs, or with their cable TV service canceled, or whatever changes they had made due to the recession. They wrote about the silver linings they found in their troubles and the many blessings in their lives. We had so many fabulous stories that included the phrase "count your blessings" that we decided to make a book by that title, which we published just four months later.

> *Scientific studies have proven that people who practice gratitude in their daily lives are happier, healthier, and more successful.*

When we decided to make our *Count Your Blessings* book, we had already selected eighty-five stories for it from the ones that had been submitted for the *Tough Times* book. We only needed sixteen more stories to get to our magic number of 101. So we sent an e-mail to our past contributors, letting them know what we needed and giving them only two weeks to submit. We received almost 2,000 submissions in those two weeks, a record number of daily submissions for a single book. We had struck a chord. Our writers know all about counting their blessings, which is probably why I like them so much!

Grateful people are more fun. No one likes a complainer, and everyone loves an upbeat, optimistic person. Perhaps that's why scientific studies have proven that people who practice gratitude in their daily lives are happier, healthier, and more successful in their work and their relationships. We ended up taking most of those 2,000 submissions from our grateful, happy writers and rolling them over for consideration for a third volume, our big bestseller *Chicken Soup for the Soul: Think Positive.*

That trio of books — *Tough Times, Tough People, Count Your Blessings,* and *Think Positive* — makes me very happy. Those books embody all that is good about human beings and about our mission to help people through sharing real-life personal stories from their peers.

The wonderful thing about counting your blessings or practicing gratitude is that you don't have to be *born* that way. You can *learn* how to be a thankful person and enjoy the benefits of gratitude.

We have hundreds of stories that teach you *how* to count your blessings, see the silver linings, put life's ups and downs in perspective, and harness the power of gratitude in your own life. As Deborah Norville says in her introduction to our latest book, *Chicken Soup for the Soul: The Power of Gratitude*, "The good news is you can *become* more grateful even if it doesn't come naturally for you. Hearing other people's stories of gratitude is one way to do it."

Deborah and I have worked on four books. She was the foreword writer for two — *Chicken Soup for the Soul: Think Positive* and *Chicken Soup for the Soul: Find Your Happiness* — and my coauthor on the next two, *Chicken Soup for the Soul: Think Possible* and our latest, *Chicken Soup for the Soul: The Power of Gratitude*. This photo shows us at the Stamford, Connecticut library, where Deborah made a presentation about the *Think Possible* book after it came out in the fall of 2015.

I was so pleased to work with her on our gratitude book as this is an area of special interest to Deborah, who is not only a journalist and the host of *Inside Edition*, but also the author of the New York Times Best Seller on the topic — *Thank You Power: Making the Science of Gratitude Work for You.*

"We can only be said to be alive in those moments when our hearts are conscious of our treasures," said American playwright and novelist Thornton Wilder. That's what counting your blessings does — it keeps you energized and participating in the world with vim and vigor. And the great thing is that it's something you can easily do, just by *deciding*. Let me give you a few examples of how you can use the power of gratitude and count your blessings. Let's start with one of my favorite stories on *deliberately* practicing thankfulness, by Ruth Jones, from *Chicken Soup for the Soul: Find Your Happiness*.

In "The Great Thanksgiving Challenge," Ruth describes how she and her friend Marilyn were sitting in a coffee shop complaining about everything they had to do. Marilyn was bemoaning all the preparation required to have her friends over for her book group meeting, and Ruth was dreading the work required to have her family come for Thanksgiving. She and Marilyn listed what that meant: "Cooking and cleaning, changing sheets, wondering what to feed everybody for breakfast."

Then a bedraggled woman entered the coffee shop, obviously homeless. Marilyn headed for the counter and paid for the woman's breakfast. When Ruth complimented her, Marilyn said, "That was guilt."

Ruth realized that she and Marilyn had fallen into a bad habit of complaining about their lives, which were full of family and friends, nice homes and good food. "We should stop complaining — it's a bad habit," she said. They decided to give up complaining for Thanksgiving.

Marilyn laid out their challenge: "We'll keep a diary. Write down every complaint. Then think of something to be thankful for, and write that down too."

The next morning Ruth called Marilyn. "I've been awake fifteen minutes and all I've done is complain," she admitted. "This is hard!"

Marilyn laughed. "Okay—quick—what are you thankful for?"

"I'm talking on the phone with my best friend and the cat is purring in my lap. What about you?"

"I'm drinking coffee in a warm kitchen and about to go work out," Marilyn answered. "See? This won't be so hard after all."

Ruth wrote, "It was hard to believe I complained so much about trivial things. Hard to believe I wasn't more thankful for my family, my friends, and my health. My mind kept wandering back to the homeless woman."

As the weeks passed, Ruth and Marilyn noticed they were recording more blessings than complaints in their notebooks. They had better attitudes and they were looking forward to the rest of the holiday season. Counting your blessings works! As Gerald Good said, "If you want to turn your life around, try thankfulness. It will change your life mightily."

***

Besides being grateful for what we have, as Marilyn and Ruth learned to do, we can also teach ourselves to approach new situations with gratitude, with the intention to find joy in them even if we don't see a sliver of silver lining at first.

In "The Unexpected Detour," which we published in *Count Your Blessings*, Dayle Allen Shockley describes how she pulled herself out of a pessimistic mindset during a family vacation in order to focus on the blessings around her.

Dayle and her husband, Stan, were on a summer road trip with their young daughter to the Great Smoky Mountains along the Tennessee/North Carolina border when Stan smelled something burning. After pulling their worn-out van and pop-up camper over at a rest area, Stan opened the hood and identified the problem: a bad oil leak.

Dayle immediately went into misery mode.

"It's always something," she muttered to herself. If only Stan had listened to her earlier, when she'd said she didn't think their old van was up for the trip. After all, it had 200,000 miles on it.

"But, being the eternal optimist that he is," Dayle continues, "my husband's faith proved stronger than my doubts. And now, here we sat on the side of the road, a sad little bunch. So much for optimism."

The trio drove slowly to the next town, stopping every few miles to add oil. Dayle's mood plummeted with each mile they drove. It was hours later and already dark when they reached Noccalula Falls Park and Campground outside Gadsden, Alabama. They would spend the night there and look for an auto shop in the morning.

> "If you want to turn your life around, try thankfulness. It will change your life mightily."

In the morning, Dayle woke to a delicious smell. She peeked out through the canvas flap and saw her husband frying bacon in a skillet with four eggs sitting beside him ready to go in next. He smiled and said he was "making the best of a bad situation." Over breakfast, he handed her brochures for local sightseeing. His idea was for the family to take in the sights while the car was in the shop getting fixed.

Dayle was impressed by her husband's optimism. The last thing she felt like doing was sightseeing. How could her husband always roll with the punches? He wanted the family to enjoy their little detour, but Dayle had no such intention. When Stan returned later that day in a rental car, with the news that their van needed expensive repairs, she decided the whole trip had been a big mistake.

The next morning, she gloomily set off on the sightseeing excursion. But as they hiked and explored the area, which lay at the foot of the Appalachian Mountains, it was difficult for Dayle to stay miserable amid the enchanting, unspoiled beauty of waterfalls, trails, gorges, and beautiful stone monuments.

"As we navigated the slippery trail, I paused in a mossy clearing and looked up," says Dayle. "Out of the frothy spray of the waterfall, giant cedars and evergreens rose up like fluted columns and, overhead, yellow sunlight winked through a canopy of leafy branches." Stan commented on how beautiful it was and Dayle had to agree. She was suddenly mesmerized, saying, "It is absolutely gorgeous."

More hiking took them around winding pines and to the top of straw-covered hills. As Dayle stood atop one of the hills and looked down at the valley below, she took a deep breath.

"I sensed a lightness of heart, as if this were the place I should be," she says.

That night at supper, the mood was upbeat.

"We couldn't stop talking about the enjoyable day we had spent together, and the spectacular beauty that was ours for the taking," admits Dayle. "Had our trip stayed on course, we never would have seen this delightful place. Noccalula Falls remains one of our all-time favorite places, and it was there I learned a valuable lesson: No matter where the road may take me, I won't let an unexpected detour spoil the day. Instead, I will follow its impulsive path to the sunlight and shadows just waiting to be discovered in serendipitous places."

* * *

Some of us learn to use the power of gratitude early in our lives and for some of us it even comes naturally. We each have different traits that are stronger in us. For me, gratitude is one of the strong ones. I almost always feel lucky and privileged and thankful for what I have. And that makes my days much brighter. But even then, it's easy to get used to our luxuries and take them for granted. I do lose perspective occasionally.

One time that stands out for me was when we were in the middle of the Peruvian highlands in the Andes on one of those blended-family vacations I mentioned in Chapter 12. There we were, in a little shack where a local artisan was selling ceramic pitchers he had baked in a wood-fired kiln. Most of the local residents in the area lived in one-room houses, some without electricity.

I picked up one of the artisan's exquisite, handmade creations and asked: "Um, excuse me, but is this dishwasher-safe?"

Because I was going to use the little pitcher, with an Incan figure on it, for maple syrup.

For pancakes.

And I didn't want to wash it by hand afterwards.

You can't get more "Ugly American" than that!

The artisan and our tour guide looked at me, confused. Yes, I could wash the pitchers. Why would I think they weren't washable? The concept of an *automated* dishwasher eluded them. I realized my mistake immediately, bought two red-clay ceramic pitchers, and reminded myself that 90% of the world didn't use a dishwasher

 and had never heard of such a thing.

This was in 2003, in an area of Peru where the vast majority of the tourists were hikers, as we were. But even though the people had few possessions, everyone had food and shelter and clothing; everyone was friendly, and there was no crime at all against tourists. The children were inspiring, clad in neat school uniforms and walking miles back and forth to school each day through the steep foothills.

People seemed happy and productive and healthy. They didn't

need dishwashers. No one really *needs* a dishwasher. Life was simpler, more grounded, more self-sufficient. And it made me feel spoiled, privileged, and pretty wasteful.

Ironically, the day before we were to leave for Peru, August 14, 2003, was when that huge blackout had occurred, the one that knocked out power to ten million people in Ontario and forty-five million people in the U.S. We had scrambled to find a new flight to Peru on the 15th, driving from New York's shutdown JFK airport all the way to Boston, discovering miraculous pockets of electricity in Massachusetts so that we could fill our empty gas tank, and staying in Boston overnight. We managed to fly to Peru from Boston on the 16th, a day late for our tour and with renewed awareness of our dependence on modern conveniences.

I've traveled all over the world since I was a kid, from highly developed countries in Europe, Asia, and the Middle East to Third World countries in South and Central America, and in Africa. I've visited forty-two countries so far — some for weeks or months, some for only a day, and many of them repeatedly over the years. They have all been beautiful and exotic and fascinating. All of them have opened my mind and made me aware of how fortunate I am to live in a First World country.

We don't have to go through armed border crossings to drive from one state to another; we can move freely about our vast territory without government interference and live and work wherever we want; we can go to college even if our parents did not; women have (mostly) equal rights; and most of us live in places where we don't wake up every morning wondering what danger the day will bring. Nothing beats our standard of living, our freedom of choice, our ease of movement, and above all, our opportunity to prosper.

I think one of the best things I did for my kids was taking them on as many international trips, including to less developed countries, as possible. That travel opened their eyes to the same things — and they gained some perspective on how good they had it growing up in a pretty fancy American town.

I kid you not, every single morning I stand in the shower and I think about those Andean highlands in Peru. I am grateful for my shower with its unlimited hot water, my clean towels, and the unbelievable luxury of the way that we live. I think about those kids walking miles to go to school as I get in my comfortable car to go to work.

Counting my blessings is my constant state of being.

A Field Full of Wishes

Redefine anything and make it better

talked about gratitude in the previous chapter and how helpful and healthy it is for us. But can you force a person to feel it and practice it? I remember a time I wanted to force-feed some gratitude to another person, but I didn't. I still regret it.

I had just exited my car to go into the grocery store when a woman about my age rolled her shopping cart up to the SUV next to mine and started loading her bags into the back. It was during the Christmas holidays, when almost every woman is busy busy busy. She was chanting: "All they do is eat. It's the same thing over and over again. It never ends. Every day is the same."

She kept on complaining in the same vein. And she wasn't *pretending* to be upset, the way women sometimes complain about how much they have to do but you know they're secretly pleased to be caring for their loved ones. This crabby woman was angry and stressed and resentful and she was venting to a complete stranger: me.

I wanted to say, "You are so lucky that you have money to buy food 'over and over again' and that you have a nice car to carry that food home for you. You are lucky that you have people waiting at home who love you, who depend on you and are healthy enough to eat 'over and over again.'"

And because she was my age, I assumed that she was probably talking about a husband and grown kids, I wanted to add, "Don't you remember why you married that man and had those children? You wanted them. You signed up for this. And you love those hungry people who have come home to visit."

But I didn't say a thing. I chickened out. I only had a second to make the decision and I thought I was being presumptuous. Even though I've published stories about people having epiphanies when a total stranger says the right words to them, and even though I've read hundreds of stories from women in similar circumstances, and even though I thought I was right, I didn't have the right to point out the obvious to a stranger.

I have a front row seat in the lives of our writers and I think I can tell when someone needs an attitude adjustment. But I did that diffident thing I occasionally do and I kept my mouth shut. The journalist Sydney J. Harris said, "Regret for the things we did can be tempered by time; it is regret for the things we did not do that is inconsolable."

> Dandelions ≠ weeds.
> Dandelions = wishes.

I should have spoken up. Maybe I could have made a difference. Maybe I could have pushed her "reset button" with a few choice words. She might have lashed out at me, and then I would have regretted opening my mouth. But at least I would regret that I *took* action, instead of regretting my *inaction*.

It's all about definition, right? When my house is full of people during the holidays, I am running around like a chicken with its head cut off, and I am stressed beyond words because I still have all my "work" work *plus* a house full of people. But it's a good stress, the kind that comes from a full and wondrous life. I know that I have *chosen* to do all these things, so how can I complain about them?

You've got to "think positive." Almost anything can be redefined. Just like that starfish story that I told you in Chapter 1, the one that was so incredibly simple, here's another simple but highly effective one, from *Chicken Soup for the Soul: Think Positive*. This story had a big impact on me:

Weeds
by Kathi Lessner Schafer

My four-year-old daughter Kristina and I were late again. I had our faded blue minivan going as fast as our town's streets allowed, but we still got stuck at every red light and didn't make it through the final intersection in time to beat the school buses exiting the high school parking lot. So there we sat for a long time.

The grassy field beside us was a sea of dandelions—not the yellow flowers, but the white fluffy ones.

I said, "Oh Kristina, that poor yard... look at all those weeds," to which she replied "Oh, Mommy, look at all those wishes!"

I love that story. Dandelions ≠ weeds. Dandelions = wishes waiting to be made by a little girl picking them and blowing those fluffy white seeds all over the place, planting more wishes!

My kids sometimes accuse me of "rationalizing" things. But I don't think it's *rationalizing* to look for a better way to see things, to *redefine* them into something more palatable, even something exciting and good. That just seems *rational* to me.

***

Here's a great example of how redefining something can transform it:

My friend Karen was having a problem with an unwanted obligation. She and her husband David were acquainted with an elderly lady, Rose, who fell ill and had no one to help her. Karen and David weren't related to Rose but since there was no one else, they stepped in and acted like family.

And Rose was difficult. She would take them out for dinner but then restrict what they were allowed to order. She would complain about everything they did for her even though they were just trying to help.

Karen and David helped Rose for a couple of years, moving her into an assisted living facility, overseeing her medical care, taking her out for meals, and then moving her again, into a nursing home. They were driving two hours each way to tend to Rose's needs and it was cutting into their workdays and their time with their children and grandchildren.

Karen and David are the nicest people you've ever met, so generous with their time and their money, but even they felt increasingly overwhelmed. They weren't resentful, but they did feel that this obligation had taken over their lives. After all, Rose was just an acquaintance. How did they get stuck with this?

> *"If you don't like something, change it; if you can't change it, change the way you think about it."*

One day, Karen was telling me how hard this was. I asked her if she did any volunteer work. She said that she would like to but that she didn't have time. I suggested that she view caring for Rose as her volunteer work.

It was like a light bulb went on. Karen's attitude was transformed instantly. She didn't need to do any less for Rose, but now that she was "volunteering" her perception of the work shifted. Karen told David what I said that night — that this was their "volunteer work" — and she called me back to say that this changed everything for him, too.

For the rest of Rose's life, Karen and David happily did their "volunteer work."

There's a great quote from the writer and artist Mary Engelbreit, who said, "If you don't like something, change it; if you can't change it, change the way you think about it." It certainly worked for Karen and David.

Now here's the surprise ending: In her will, Rose left Karen and David almost half a million dollars. They had come to terms with caring for her, were doing it willingly as their volunteer work, and then got a huge, unexpected reward for their kindness when it was all said and done.

***

We talk a lot about volunteering at Chicken Soup for the Soul. We've published a couple of books specifically on the topic and we have stories about volunteering sprinkled throughout all our books, probably because our writers are a nice bunch of people, but also because volunteering makes us *feel* good, and we're all about stories that make us feel good.

The biggest *beneficiary* of volunteering is usually the person *doing* the volunteering, not the *recipient* of the work. Therapists often recommend that people who are depressed or even suicidal take up volunteer work as a way of showing themselves that they add value to society, that what they do makes a difference.

What I'm suggesting is that you go one step further and do what Karen and David did — redefine some extra help you are giving or work that you are doing as "volunteering." That way, a task that you feel *forced* to do can turn into *voluntary* volunteering.

Here's my own example. I serve as the treasurer for my neighborhood tax district, which basically means that I run it. I carve out many hours each month to serve as the tax assessor, tax collector, bill payer, and tax return preparer and I also manage the garbage collection and some other services for the whole neighborhood. There are nineteen homes, and while almost everyone is wonderful, there are always a few people who are difficult. I can't hand the job off to anyone either, because it requires a lot of financial skills, which I have from my decades on Wall Street. I've been doing this somewhat thankless job in my neighborhood for at least eighteen years now.

A few years ago, someone asked me if I did volunteer work and I said, "No, because I am so busy with work and our four grown kids and a house and running my neighborhood association that I don't have time to do volunteer work." And then I realized, "Oh! Running the association is my volunteer work." And that changed everything. It's my *volunteer work.*

So now, when I get aggravated over someone complaining about the snowplowing, or a tree falling across the road, or Anger Management Guy not paying his neighborhood taxes, I remind myself that this is my volunteer work and it seems much more palatable.

That almost always works, except when it didn't, a couple of winters ago, when a few of the neighbors were driving "volunteer me" crazy with complaints. We had something like six feet of snow in one month, plus lots of freezing rain. You had to hold onto your car to get your mail from the mailbox without falling over as the roads were covered with black ice.

One woman called and complained there was ice in her driveway after we had two feet of snow in one week. *Duh.* Another neighbor refused to leave his driveway gate open and then complained when he wasn't plowed first. He had me up at five in the morning texting the snowplow guy. And then there was Mrs. Anger Management Guy, who complained that the plow was pushing snow onto the landscaping on the edge of her driveway. As if snow could be miraculously transported into space instead of *pushed* to the side of her driveway!

I was going crazy that winter. My colleagues at work would constantly hear me on the phone fielding complaints and talking to the snowplow guy. Ernest Hemingway said that all poets are crazy and I get it now. I had to express my angst and I turned to poetry. Despite the fact that I had *never, ever* voluntarily written a poem, I sat down and composed eight haikus — in classic five-syllable seven-syllable five-syllable format — about the snowplowing situation, some less polite than others, and e-mailed them off to my friends who helped manage our neighborhood association. Here are four of them:

one more dumb complaint
about snow, ice, and slipping
and there will be blood

paternalistic
society not the plan
so let's grow up now

shrubs and lights you put
along driveway go under
snow as you designed

only one person
can go first in the real world
despite what you wish

My "good" neighbors wrote back that they were laughing out loud. It was a way of venting and getting my frustration out of my system, true. But it was also a creative way to redefine and refocus that frustration. After all, our mothers always said, "Use your words."

And along with our Chicken Soup for the Soul readers and writers, I've discovered that with words and thoughts, almost anything can be redefined, turned upside down and inside out, and re-examined in a new light.

CHAPTER
—17—

A Good Deed a Day

*Do this and the biggest beneficiary
will be you*

Just as our writers tell us that writing down a blessing a day keeps them happy, and that doing volunteer work fulfills them, we hear all the time that doing good deeds is a surefire way to make you feel great.

Your first foray into doing a good deed today could be that smile you bestow on a stranger as a result of reading Chapter 2. Or it could be when you speak up on behalf of someone who's being mistreated, like in Chapter 8. Whatever you do, and whenever it happens, I bet there will be a spring in your step after you do a good deed for someone.

In Chapter 10, we saw how Esther Griffin reacted when she was told that she had only one year left to live. One of the things that she did, because she was searching for great meaning in that year, was to volunteer. When Esther was confronted with her own mortality in her mid-fifties that was her focus—she wanted to help others.

***

Since helping others makes us feel good, why not do a little bit of that every day? Here's a little motivation, courtesy of Shannon Anderson. Her story, "A Deed a Day," was published in *Chicken Soup for the Soul: Find Your Happiness*.

As Shannon describes it, one evening she was cooking and

doing laundry, the kids were squabbling over whose turn it was to let out the dog, and her husband was annoyed that dinner wasn't on the table yet. Everyone was in their own little silo, caring about their particular lives and tasks.

Shannon was upset that night. She explains: "We had become absorbed in our own activities and not very considerate toward those around us. We needed to do something to bring back some meaning into our lives. It needed to be something that would refocus our own agendas and energize us toward the common good."

So Shannon purchased a journal, labeled it "Our Deed Diary" and held a family meeting. She told her husband and daughters that

> *Who would have thought that trying to do a simple kindness a day would be so rewarding?*

she wanted them to start doing something kind every day. That good deed could be for another family member *or* for someone outside their home. The purpose was to reduce the focus on themselves and brighten someone else's day in the process.

The family defined a good deed as doing something unexpected for someone else. It could be as simple as making a card for a teacher or giving someone a compliment. Shannon and her husband and children would discuss their good deeds over dinner each night and record them in their deed journal.

Shannon says it was harder than you might think to come up with their good deeds each day. Remember, it had to be something they didn't normally do. So if they normally sent someone a birthday card, that didn't count. If the girls normally helped their mom with a certain chore, that didn't count. These had to be *new* good deeds, outside of their normal lives.

After a few weeks they got the hang of it, and Shannon says it has made a difference: "Instead of always wondering what the day will bring for us, we think about what we can do for someone else. At dinner, we have an instant conversation starter, as we all share our stories."

Shannon expanded the good deed experiment to her first-grade classroom. The kids began by writing thank-you letters to the people who worked in the school. Shannon says, "It was most touching to observe the janitor, nurse, librarian, and other school staff hang our notes on their walls while beaming because they felt appreciated."

The class as a whole tried to do three good deeds per day, and it transformed the kids. "When a student spills his or her crayons, you wouldn't believe how many kids scurry over to try to help and clean them up!" reports Shannon. "Just as with my family, keeping and sharing a Deed Diary changed our whole outlook on life. Who would have thought that trying to do a simple kindness a day would be so rewarding?"

I love that story. What an easy way to change a family dynamic, invigorate a classroom, and instill lasting values in kids. And kids or not, what a great way for you to brighten your own days. You don't even have to write down your good deeds. You merely have to decide each day to do one little thing for someone else — open a door, pick up a piece of trash, let a mother with a squirming kid go ahead of you in line at the store, or pick up an extra coffee for someone at work.

The famous basketball coach John Wooden had this to say: "You can't live a perfect day without doing something for someone who will never be able to repay you." That is indeed the best kind of good deed, one you do with no thought of personal benefit.

***

But sometimes those good deeds *do* end up directly benefiting you! LaVerne Otis, who has written many wonderful stories for us on a variety of topics, did a good deed that ended up changing her life. In her story, "Bus Stop Blessing," which we published in

Chicken Soup for the Soul: Count Your Blessings, she tells us about the time she gave a ride to a young woman who had missed the bus. LaVerne saw the woman running as fast as she could, and then collapsing on the bus bench in tears after the driver failed to stop for her.

It was the first day of LaVerne's vacation and she was on her way to the mall, but something about the young woman compelled her to pull over and offer some comfort. LaVerne sat on the bench next to her and gently mentioned that another bus would be along in half an hour or so. She introduced herself and asked, "What's your name?"

"My name is Sarah. I'm sorry to make such a scene but I need to get to the hospital to be with my sick baby," she responded. Sarah explained that she was a single mother and that her one-year-old son was in the hospital with pneumonia. Her car battery was dead and that's why she was taking the bus. Now, this young, overwhelmed mother worried that her baby would be frightened without her.

LaVerne gave Sarah a ride to the hospital. She also arranged for her brother to help Sarah with her car battery that night. Then LaVerne shared Sarah's plight with her Bible study group and they donated baby clothing and some money to Sarah.

The best thing that came from LaVerne's good deed was that her brother fell in love with Sarah, who is now LaVerne's sister-in-law and a precious addition to her life!

Good deeds can indeed have a big impact. In *The Merchant of Venice*, Shakespeare wrote, "How far that little candle throws his beams! So shines a good deed in a weary world."

***

I've been talking about doing good deeds for altruistic reasons, but there is also another way to look at good deeds — as useful tools to change human behavior. That's how Andrew Nalian used them, as he tells us in "The Good Deed Challenge," which we published in *Chicken Soup for the Soul: Find Your Inner Strength*.

Andrew had just graduated from Central Michigan University, and he wanted to travel a bit. So he got a summer job as a server on a cruise ship in Alaska. He was going for the last months of the season, a very competitive time for servers to try to make as much money as possible before the tourist season was over. Therefore, Andrew's arrival as a newbie was not welcomed and he found himself in a hostile environment, subject to a lot of workplace bullying.

> *"Good actions give strength to ourselves and inspire good actions in others."*

On a cruise ship you can't exactly get away from your colleagues either. Everyone lives together. Andrew was pretty miserable, stuck on a ship with awful cell phone reception, no friends, and the bullies.

There were two bullies in particular who tried to make Andrew unhappy enough to quit. If he even spoke to them, they'd snap back at him, and one of them even became physically abusive. Andrew thought about quitting every day but he didn't do it. He was smart and determined and he knew that this was his opportunity to solve his own problem.

Andrew decided to analyze what was motivating the bullies. He knew that bitterness and disappointment can drive someone to become a bully. The main bully, for example, was thirty-one, much older than the rest of the employees, who were mostly of college age. That must have been uncomfortable for him, and he might have felt that life was passing him by.

He also noticed that the very first time the main bully made a mean comment to him, he got laughs from the others. Andrew realized that picking on others was the method this bully used to make friends for himself.

"If he hurt one person to make five others laugh, he was winning," explains Andrew. "My goal was to change this habit and outlook."

Andrew decided to start a good deed project. It was a bit of an experiment, but as I said, Andrew was impressively analytical about the whole situation. He decided to do a good deed every day for the bullies, especially one in particular. He opened the door for him when he saw him, and he did everything he could to make the bully's life easier.

Soon, Andrew relates, "I noticed he stopped acting as rude and hateful. As I did these good deeds, I studied how my bully's persona would change from an individual setting to a group setting."

The bully's friends took note. One of them told Andrew, "You don't deserve the way people are treating you; you deserve better than this." Andrew started making friends with all the main bully's friends, and that was the final turning point: he couldn't very well bully Andrew anymore while they were hanging out with mutual friends.

The main bully now gave Andrew respect, and he finished off his job in much better circumstances than he had started. He had a new mission in life as well: to spread the message about how good deeds can change everything. His book, *50 Deeds for Those in Need*, came out in 2013 to excellent reviews. It contains a wonderful list of suggested good deeds, and I'll pass on a few from the table of contents:

- Chalk a motivational message on the sidewalk
- Donate blood
- Write a positive online review
- Bring in your neighbor's trashcans
- Become an organ donor
- Thank someone in uniform

- Help someone whose car has broken down
- Return a shopping cart

Whatever our inspiration for doing a good deed, the great news is that once the deed is done, it isn't over and it isn't really done — it multiplies into other heartfelt deeds as the goodness travels. Good deeds are as contagious as a smile.

You know we like our inspirational quotes at Chicken Soup for the Soul, so here comes another one, from Plato. It does a great job of summing up what we learned from Shannon, LaVerne, and Andrew: "Good actions give strength to ourselves and inspire good actions in others."

Use the Guest Soap

Live it up — enjoy those little pleasures every day

Y ou just finished reading about doing a good deed a day for family members, friends, colleagues, or total strangers. Now let's talk about doing a good deed for yourself.

Think about how often we deprive ourselves of simple, little pleasures that would brighten our days at little or no cost. What is it that makes us think that self-sacrifice all the time is good?

My husband, for example, used to go to the bagel shop every day on his way to work when he commuted to New York City. Bill grew up in Brooklyn and he's a bagel aficionado as a result. His favorite kind of bagel is an "everything" bagel, coated with salt, onion flakes, sesame seeds, and poppy seeds. But for some reason, Bill would only order an "everything" bagel on weekends. He didn't allow himself to have one during the week. They cost the same amount as any other kind of bagel — not a penny more — and they take the exact same amount of time to prepare. So I finally convinced him that he could eat "everything" bagels whenever he wanted — it was a revelation to him!

One of our slogans at Chicken Soup for the Soul is that we are "changing your life one story at a time" and that includes stories that give you quick and easy tips. These are stories that don't require you to do anything more than *deciding*. You don't have to take a course, fill out a journal, sweat, or do anything! In this case, all you have to do is *decide* to stop depriving yourself of the good stuff, the special occasion stuff, the stuff that you save for *other* people. In other words, use the guest soap!

* * *

One of my favorite and most convincing stories on this topic is called "Guest Treatment" and it's by Paula Klendworth Skory. We published it in *Chicken Soup for the Soul: Time to Thrive*, which was filled with examples of how you can make your life better with little tweaks… like not saving the nice soap for your guests.

I think Paula was raised the way most of us were. She says her mom had guest soaps in the bathroom, and you've probably seen what she describes—those tiny green and pink and yellow roses that sit around for so long that they get kind of gross, with brown lines in all the crevices of the petals.

> *It amazes me how often we all deprive ourselves of those simple, little pleasures that would brighten our days at little or no cost.*

You probably don't have the little soap roses now, but you might have some other kind of newfangled guest soap. It might be one of those soaps that looks like a piece of marble, or a fancy scented one that you received as a gift, or an expensive French liquid soap, one that is "too good" for everyday use. That's what I have—a bottle of L'Occitane liquid soap in the powder room—something I would never treat myself to in my own bathroom or the kitchen.

Paula had one of those nice soaps that look like a piece of rock, a chunk of green marbled glycerin, lightly scented and wrapped in cellophane with a lovely label proclaiming that it had been handcrafted by her new brother-in-law. That soap was so nice and smelled so good that she wanted to save it. Save it for what? I don't know. And neither did Paula.

Paula put it in her scarf drawer and used it as a sachet. It stayed there for years, as she progressed from new bride to young mother to mother of teens to empty nester. Paula was still saving the soap even when the kids had been gone long enough that she converted one of their bedrooms into a craft room. She used the soap as a decoration in there.

Then Paula got cancer and the craft room turned into her recovery room. As she recuperated, she started to take inventory of her life and her surroundings. And she noticed that special soap sitting there, still waiting for her to be special enough to use it.

Cancer has a way of cutting through nonsense. And making people treat themselves better. Even as well as a guest!

Paula carefully unwrapped the soap, which still smelled great even after decades of being saved. She put that soap under running water and it came to life. And then Paula left her hands there, making soap foam, and let all her troubles wash away. She said it was "a small moment of pure joy." She felt pampered and loved. She couldn't believe that she had waited all those years to use the special soap.

Paula says that cancer may have been an unwelcome guest in her life, but this is one of the good things that came from that visit. From now on she will use the guest soap… and the good towels too. Yeah, I know. You don't use those either.

That story made an impression on me. I'm trying to be better now about using the nice things in the house. I'm even thinking of moving the good china so that it's as easy to pull out as the everyday plates. Maybe when I finish writing this book…

I definitely *should* sit myself down and make at least five changes in my life based on all the tips in this book, right? I did that after I edited *Chicken Soup for the Soul: The Joy of Less*, which was about de-cluttering your life. I took carloads of clothing and shoes and coats and boots to the thrift shop so that someone else could benefit from them, and I love how much lighter and freer I feel now.

***

Here's another easy-to-implement tip for you, from a story by Elaine Bridge called "Every Day a Friday." It was published in *Chicken Soup for the Soul: Think Positive.*

Elaine tells us that she would always celebrate Fridays. She would drop off her son at school, pick up a fancy coffee at Starbucks, and then take a longer route home — a more scenic road — sipping her fancy coffee. She would find herself smiling all day because it was Friday and Fridays were special.

Later in the day, Elaine would pick up her son at school, and they would drive around noticing all the signs of Friday celebration in their college town — the kids out on the lawns, the parties starting up. Everyone loves Fridays.

But then one day Elaine had a doctor's appointment and got good news about a medical situation she had been worrying about. She came out of that doctor's office happy and relieved and noticing all the signs of spring around her — flowers blossoming, birds singing, bright sunshine warming her back.

She was ready to celebrate, and what better way than a cappuccino? But it was Tuesday. And special coffee was reserved for Friday.

"Suddenly I realized how ridiculous that line of thinking was!" says Elaine. "Why should Fridays be any more special than any other day of the week? Why waste six days while waiting to rejoice on the seventh?"

A few minutes later, Elaine was walking back to her car with a big grin on her face and a special coffee in her hand.

After she turned her Tuesday into a Friday, with that special coffee, Elaine had an epiphany. And she wrote the following: "It's how many of us live our lives. We're waiting for conditions to be right before we allow ourselves to enjoy our time here on earth. We'll rejoice when the car is paid off, or enjoy life when we're finally able to retire. And in that waiting we waste so much of life and the happiness that can be found in our todays. What if we moved a little of that 'Friday feeling' into our rainy-day Mondays, our gloomy Tuesdays and our mid-week Wednesdays?"

She is so right. Go for it. Choose your own little thing and make every day a Friday.

***

Sometimes you have to throw caution to the wind and treat yourself to something even bigger than a fancy coffee. Because that's what adds spice to your life. I remember one time, when I was taking the kids to Disney World, my assistant made a suggestion that I initially rejected.

The plan was to pick up the kids after school in one of those black airport sedans and whisk them off for a surprise trip to Disney World. I was making it a surprise because a previous, *announced* trip to Disney World had been canceled due to a business obligation. I didn't want to disappoint the kids again. So this time, I wouldn't say a word. I would send them off to school and pack their bags once they were out of the house. Then the car would pick me up at home and we would pick up the kids at school and proceed to LaGuardia Airport.

My assistant had discovered that for only $10 more I could get a stretch limousine instead of a regular sedan. I said no. But then I realized how much fun it would be for the kids. And it was all of $10 more. I picked them up at school in that stretch limo, took them to the local McDonald's, and then we went on our way to the airport. It was a big thrill for all of us.

So when I read "The Muscle Car" by Janet Bower I totally understood. We published her story in *Chicken Soup for the Soul:*

Time to Thrive, which is filled with stories about people figuring out all those little ways to enjoy their time more, to fulfill their desires, and to live happier.

When Janet's car was damaged by a valet service, it had to go to the body shop. She had to rent a car for five days and even though she and her husband were in their seventies, she figured, "Why not?" and she rented a Camaro. It's obvious why Janet and Bob had already been married for forty-six years at that time. This is a couple that knows how to have fun.

Janet asked Enterprise Rent-A-Car if they had a black one with red flames trimmed with gold on the hood, but had to settle for a plain black one. Nevertheless, it was a Camaro, and they were going to have a blast… after they figured out how to maneuver their rather inflexible bodies under the rather low roof into those rather narrow seats. The next challenge was closing the giant doors, which Janet said required seven-foot arms.

> "We don't stop playing because we grow old; we grow old because we stop playing."

Then they were off, and Janet says, "By driving fast, we managed to look almost like we belonged in a Camaro. By the time admiring observers realized how old we were, we were gone."

Bob and Janet drove all over their local area—San Diego County, which is huge, about the size of my little state of Connecticut. They drove in the mountains, which are more than 6,000 feet high, and they drove along the shimmering beaches of Coronado and La Jolla. As they drove up a mountain road the first day, passing stands of pine trees, farms, and cattle, their "muscle car" clung to the curves and they felt its power as it devoured those steep hills like they weren't there.

The car was just as much fun when they purred through downtown La Jolla and San Diego, even when they got lost. Janet and Bob drove everywhere, and they also visited numerous acclaimed restaurants and shopped in their black Camaro.

George Bernard Shaw said, "We don't stop playing because we grow old; we grow old because we stop playing." Those septuagenarians had quite an adventure, all because they took the opportunity to "tweak" that rental car a bit. They needed to get a rental anyway, so why not make it an occasion? Janet says they had "the fun, excitement, and challenge that two elderly, long-married people can have but seldom do. There are always routines and schedules, but there are also new opportunities. When those opportunities arise, take them — at any age."

***

So that's it. Use the guest soap. Get an "everything" bagel. Treat yourself to that special coffee. Upgrade your airport ride for $10. And rent a Camaro when your car gets crunched. These are all easy ways to live it up a little. You deserve it.

The Power of No

De-clutter your calendar and home to make room for what matters

N ow that you've decided to treat yourself as well as you would treat a guest, and you've decided to enjoy those simple, little pleasures you had been forgoing, let's talk about "me" time. You need that, too. But if you're like me, you have too much to do and you're always trying to reclaim control of your calendar so that you can carve out time for what matters to you, whether it's a few hours with your family, friends, or downtime by yourself.

Toni Morrison said, "If there's a book that you want to read, but it hasn't been written yet, then you must write it." That happens a lot at Chicken Soup for the Soul. I am constantly coming up with new topics because I personally need to read a book on the subject! That's why we made one of our latest — *Chicken Soup for the Soul: The Joy of Less* — which has had a huge impact on me when it comes to de-cluttering my calendar and my home. The book is like an instruction manual for simplifying your life and focusing on what is most important to you.

The key is to use the Power of No. It's difficult to say at first, but once you try it, you will feel empowered to say it again and again! Sydney Logan did it, and she tells us about it in "Silencing the 'Should' Monster." She points out that many of us, particularly women, want to be *everything* to *everyone*: "We want to be the fantastic wife, amazing mother, loving daughter, caring sister, dependable employee, and supportive friend. The list is endless and exhausting."

She's right. We are always saying, "I *should* do this, I *should* do that." I talked about that a bit in Chapter 4 in the context of learning to strive for excellence instead of perfection. In her own case, Sydney was making herself miserable with all the tasks she was undertaking—keeping a sparkling clean house, cooking dinner every night, planning parties, volunteering in the community and at church, even picking out the perfect gifts for every occasion.

It was unhealthy. As Sydney explains, "Unrealistic expectations on our energy, time, and emotions can lead to anxiety, depression, guilt, and low self-esteem. Frazzled isn't just a state of mind. It's a reality." A few years ago, before Sydney learned how to say "no," that "should monster" was giving her anxiety. She went to a therapist for advice and it was very helpful. One day, she was telling the therapist about an event she was reluctantly planning to attend. The therapist said, "Why are you going if you don't want to?"

> *"Half of the troubles of this life can be traced to saying yes too quickly and not saying no soon enough."*

Sydney thought it was obvious. She said, "Because I *should*."

The therapist asked, "Why should you do something you don't want to do?" And then she went on to say, "That's why you're dealing with anxiety. You're trying to make everyone else happy. What about you? Are you happy? You have to start being a little selfish with your time. You have to learn to say no."

Well, that *does* sound obvious. But sometimes you have to hear the obvious coming out of *someone else's* mouth.

After that conversation, Sydney started saying "no" when it was possible, and she reports, "The world didn't spin off its axis." She learned how to delegate more tasks to her husband, who willingly accepted them, and she learned to say "yes" only to the things that mattered to her.

The writer Josh Billings sums it up beautifully: "Half of the troubles of this life can be traced to saying yes too quickly and not saying no soon enough."

***

I have to share this next story with you because I find it so amusing. It's also from *The Joy of Less* and it's called "From Super to Serene."

Our writer tells us that she was always trying to be Super Mom. She was a domestic goddess and the perfect mother. She did *everything* for her family. And she was finishing up her college degree, too! She often found herself doing laundry and cleaning the house in the wee hours of the morning.

Our Super Mom also volunteered. She was always getting calls to help out with this or that event, and she always said, "Yes." After all, she was always the *first person called*. It was obvious everyone needed her. So she chaperoned on field trips and she helped out in her kids' classrooms. She volunteered at church; she worked at fundraisers; she wrote newsletters.

Our poor beleaguered mother says the demands on her time were becoming overwhelming. She wasn't getting enough sleep. She didn't have enough energy. And so, one day, when she got yet another call asking for help, she did something new. She said "no."

And then she waited for the world to end.

But the woman on the other end of the phone said, "Oh, that's okay. I'm sure I can get someone else. You're the first person I've called. I just started at the top of the list."

And that's when our writer had her epiphany. Her last name starts with A. Of course she was always the first one called!

Now our Super Mom says "no" a lot more and she has become Serene Mom. And that's a whole lot better for her family.

***

I coauthored *Chicken Soup for the Soul: The Joy of Less* with Brooke Burke-Charvet, who is a very busy wife, mother of four, actress, philanthropist, and entrepreneur. She's also the host of our television show, *Chicken Soup for the Soul's Hidden Heroes*. Brooke is adamant that she spend enough time with her four kids, all of whom are still at home, so she was full of excellent advice on this topic. Her introduction to the book contained her own tale of learning how to say "no."

Brooke says, "As a young woman, I shared my life with many people aiming to please others at the expense of being true to themselves and their own needs. I'll never forget the first time my boyfriend blew off a social dinner because we were jetlagged and simply too tired to pull it off. I was so relieved that we could skip what was potentially a four-hour dinner, but I was also mortified by his insensitivity to our hosts. I remember thinking how free he must feel to not be psychologically obligated to show up for someone else's event. Rather than canceling, I have learned to say 'no' up front."

Brooke goes on to say, "I believe in the power of saying 'no'—'no' to too many material possessions, and 'no' to schedules so crowded with 'obligations' that we crowd out time we should spend with our families and our friends. We need to use the power of 'no' so that we can say 'yes' to the things that matter to us."

Our book was split evenly between stories about reducing time commitments and stories about reducing material possessions. Both are super important. One of the things that I admire about Brooke is that in addition to protecting her calendar from incursions, she goes through her closet every month, evaluating what should stay and what should go. She says, "My own rule, the result of necessity, is 'dig it or ditch it.' If you aren't using it, if you haven't worn it in a year, get it out of your life. Give it to a friend, donate it to your church or a thrift shop that supports a good cause. Someone else will value the item that no longer fits in your life."

***

The fact that you might be holding onto something in your closet or basement or garage that you will never use, and that could be of benefit to someone else, is probably the best reason of all to de-clutter your home. What really made me understand this concept was a story by Jeanie Jacobson called "Someone Else's Blessing."

Jeanie had a friend who needed help de-cluttering her home. She had a foolproof method for getting people to give away their excess stuff. She would use this line — "Are you holding onto someone else's blessing?"

That line worked great on Jeanie's friend. Because it does make sense. Why are you holding onto stuff that you don't need, that is getting in your way — and making you feel bad — when someone else could use it and enjoy it?

Jeanie's friend went through her knickknacks, clothing, purses, exercise equipment, extra bedding, and every other category of her possessions, chanting, "I refuse to hold onto someone else's blessing ever again."

Then she insisted on stuffing it all into her SUV and taking it to Goodwill right away.

After Jeanie got home from her friend's house she realized that she hadn't been following her own advice. She had a garage full of old construction material, and rooms filled with dust-covered exercise equipment, packed closets and laundry hampers, and stuffed animals that no one was playing with anymore. So she called the local thrift store to schedule a pickup.

The woman who answered asked what she would be donating.

"Blessings," Jeanie replied. "A whole bunch of blessings."

***

It's so much easier to get motivated to de-clutter when you think about how much someone else will like the things you don't need anymore. I personally have a mental image of the person who will pick up my donations from the church thrift shop. And when I'm putting clothing on hangers, finding the extra buttons that I've put away and safety-pinning them back onto shirts and sweaters, and generally making everything as nice as possible for my imaginary friend, I'm excited that these items that once were special for me will now be special for her.

I must admit that I hadn't dropped off anything at the thrift shop in a long time before this year. But after I finished reviewing the 300 finalists for the *Joy of Less* book, I was highly motivated. I realized that I was always complaining about the stuff that my grown children are still storing in my house, and that I was always needling Bill about his "souvenir T-shirt" drawer and all his college books that occupy valuable, shared bookshelf space, but that *I* wasn't exactly innocent.

> "Are you holding onto someone else's blessing?"

In a rare fit of self-awareness at the beginning of the year, lacking a New Year's resolution that I believed I'd keep, I had an epiphany. How could I justify telling my husband and children to clean up when I was just as guilty?

So I sat down at my computer during New Year's week and made a list of fifty-two de-cluttering projects to do in 2016, some big and some small.

I tried to make the projects as non-daunting as possible, cutting them into bite-size pieces to the extent that I could. I also decided I can do them in any order I want. I can even leave the most difficult ones till last. They range from the mostly easy — "clean out sock drawer and throw away the gross ones" — to the occasionally awful — "go through basement with Bill and justify every single thing in there or get rid of it."

As of mid-April I had done sixteen of the fifty-two projects.

By the way, they don't get crossed off my list until whatever I've disposed of has actually left the house... and the back of my car. That means I've already made five trips to the thrift shop, three trips to the clothing-recycling bin, and three trips to the consignment shop, to truly get rid of the stuff.

The most embarrassing, and amusing, project was when I cleaned out the cabinet in which I store pantyhose. That was one of my fifty-two projects, and it was an eye-opener. I had at least thirty pairs of white pantyhose, two-thirds of them never opened. I can't even remember when white pantyhose were last in style except on Snow White. And I found twenty pairs of navy pantyhose, too, that I have no use for now. The only survivors of any utility were the black pantyhose and tights and the skin-colored pantyhose (those may also be out of fashion right now but if you had legs as sickly white as mine you would understand). To think that I've been carting around more than one hundred pairs of pantyhose for twenty-five years, moving three times!

It took me three hours one weekend to sort through all the pantyhose and tights. And I must confess I wasted an additional thirty minutes opening the cabinet and admiring my newly labeled and organized boxes every time I walked by.

I kept thinking about Jeanie Jacobson's story while I did the project: "Are you holding onto someone else's blessing?" The longer I hold onto them, the less valuable they will be to the next person. Witness my twenty-years-out-of-style white pantyhose. It's selfish to hold onto these things that may be of benefit to someone else and it's so much wiser to get rid of them in a timely manner.

Bill got into it, too, even though I wasn't nagging him any-more about his stuff. The cold weather got him thinking and he cleaned out his coat closet and found more than a dozen men's coats and jackets — his and our son's — that I took to the thrift shop in February.

I'm excited about finishing my fifty-two projects. I already like my house better with only sixteen of the projects done. It's wonderful to open a closet and only see what I actually intend to use.

* * *

There's another approach to de-cluttering that I love, and that is to spontaneously give things away. I was the beneficiary of that when my friend Adrienne said, "Here, I bought this leather jacket in red and black and I only need one, so take the black one." Cool!

Why do people buy the same thing in multiple colors? We obviously choose our favorite color for it first, but then we don't leave well enough alone, and we buy it in another color, too. Leah Shearer Noonan wrote about that in the *Joy of Less* book. She did the same thing—if she saw something she liked, she'd buy it in more than one color, or she'd buy an extra "just in case." In case *what*? Who knows, but we all do it at times.

Then Leah got married and now she had a husband questioning why she had so many duplicate items. They needed to put away their wedding gifts and there was only so much room.

One day, her husband Patrick questioned why she had two rain jackets—one red and one green. They were very alike and both did the job. "I can't decide," Leah said sheepishly. "I love them both and I just can't decide."

A few months later, Leah's company downsized and she was offered a part-time position in lieu of the full-time one that she had held for four years. She decided to resign instead and she was driving home in the rain feeling pretty dejected. Just as she pulled off the exit ramp she saw a man cowering in the rain, drenched, and wearing only a T-shirt and jeans. He held up a pizza box on which was written "HELP ME."

Leah realized that she might have driven right by him other days. But given her mood that day she was more open to noticing him when she stopped at the red light at the end of the exit ramp.

She happened to have both rain jackets in the car. Before the light turned, she quickly rolled down the window and handed the man her beloved green jacket.

"I just barely caught the look of gratitude in his eyes before the cars beeping behind me forced me to move on," says Leah. "But I saw him mouth the words 'thank you' before wriggling into the weatherproof garment and pulling up the hood."

Leah knew he would value the jacket much more than she ever did. *Two* rain jackets in her car? She had definitely been holding onto "someone else's blessing."

Giving away her jacket was such a positive experience for Leah. "I had never been so thankful for something I gave up. Seeing that man made me feel ashamed at my own self-pity. I had a roof over my head, clothes to wear and many ways to rebound from my current misfortune. I knew when my last paycheck arrived from my job that I had savings to fall back on, and my husband was poised to help me figure out the rest."

Brooke and I met Leah at a book signing we did for *The Joy of Less* at Books and Greetings in Northvale, New Jersey.

I'm happy to report that Leah (on the left in the previous photo) loves her new job and is one happy camper. She reports that she did manage to de-clutter her home.

It does feel great to de-clutter. Try it this week. Get rid of five things and see how you like it. Excess possessions weigh us down. We don't use them and yet we have to clean them, arrange them, move them around to get to the things that we do use. They get in the way.

**

And that's why I have one more message for you from the *Joy of Less* book. It's about storage units. I know that there are some good uses for storage units: you are between homes; or you need to see how it is to live without certain things — like a test. But we were inundated with stories for our book from people who reported that they spent years paying fees for storage units and then threw everything away anyway. Here are two cautionary tales for you.

The first is called "Unit 91" and it's by Phyllis McKinley. Phyllis had moved from Maine to Jacksonville, Florida and she had way more stuff than would fit in her new home. So she rented two storage units.

Finally she got around to visiting those storage units so she could figure out what belonged in her new home. Day after day, in oppressive Florida heat and humidity, she sorted through the mess. Each unit was 360 square feet — that's like a 12x30 foot space, like two rooms of a house, and both units were filled to the ceiling.

Phyllis's mission was to sort through all this stuff. She spent weeks sorting, throwing out, making a list of things she could sell. She found a few things she wanted for the new place they were renting, but most of the stuff went right back into the storage units at the end of each day of hard labor.

Eventually, Phyllis met the owner of the storage facility and he said he would buy whatever she didn't want. After all that work, after moving all those things from Maine to Florida, she sold him most of them, including a lot of furniture that she had thought she was attached to.

Phyllis says she moved what was left into her new home, and then *continued* discarding more items and donating to Goodwill. She ended up hardly keeping any of those things she spent so much money and time moving down from Maine. "At the moment, there is nothing I need, and nothing lacking from my life," she says. "I no longer even think about all the items I got rid of nor do I miss any of them. I have no regrets, except that we moved all that stuff from Maine to Florida in the first place!"

If that story isn't enough to reform you — to make you stop hoarding, then here's another one, called "Good Riddance." In this story, Theresa Jensen Lacey, who writes as T. Jensen Lacey, tells us about *her* family's move. Her family *did* purge a lot of their possessions before they moved from one state to another. They actually had to put almost *everything* they owned in storage because they were going to rent for a few months while looking for their permanent new home. As they systematically put boxes in storage and lived with less and less in preparation for the move, Theresa says they started to feel a "sense of lightness." She realized that their possessions were really owning *them*, requiring care, cleaning, dusting, etc.

A few months later, when Theresa's family was in their permanent new home and ready to get their stuff out of storage, they didn't want it anymore. The whole family took a look into the storage unit and said almost in unison, "It's all going to Goodwill." Theresa says that was eleven years ago, and they still don't miss a single thing.

***

I hope you're inspired now to de-clutter. When you focus on all the stuff that is crowding your drawers and closets and cupboards, it starts to feel like a terrible weight. Every single de-cluttering project you do — every closet shelf you attack, every drawer you half empty, every trip you make to Goodwill — should make you feel great.

I have to say that I am eagerly looking forward to finishing this manuscript so that I can get back to my own list of fifty-two projects. I miss that feeling of accomplishment I had earlier in the year as I checked off each of those sixteen items!

Friend or Frenemy?

You have permission to remove toxic people from your life

Sometimes I think I am incredibly naïve. Can you believe that I didn't know what a "frenemy" was until six or seven years ago? I must not have watched enough Lindsay Lohan movies. As it turns out, the definition of a "frenemy" is "a friend who is actually an enemy or a rival."

I must have had a frenemy or two in the early decades of my life, but I was remarkably imperceptive about it until nine years ago when a close friend started badmouthing me behind my back *and* to my face. Imagine sitting with a group of friends and mentioning that you are going to meet your son's girlfriend for the first time, and hearing a supposed friend say, "I feel sorry for her. I wouldn't want to have *you* as *my* mother-in-law."

There were a lot of comments like that but I kept shrugging them off until I realized that my "friend" was stressing me out. It wasn't only about how she treated *me*. I was constantly hearing her snide comments about the other women in our little group, too.

My friend was making me unhappy. And friends are supposed to add value to your life, right?

I've never been jealous of a friend. I can't even imagine that! Why would I be? If a friend looks fabulous, or is extremely successful, or is more fit than I am, I just admire her and find her inspirational. She motivates me to be *better*. I love having successful, happy, beautiful friends.

I think that's why it took me so long to understand the "frenemy" concept. It hadn't been part of my experience. But once I understood it, I also understood another concept that had eluded me: "toxic people." I know, you must think that I am a total innocent. I didn't know about toxic people either!

It was working at Chicken Soup for the Soul that opened my eyes. When you read thousands of stories about friendship, and you see the good and the bad, you get a lot smarter. I also got a lot busier! And when you're super busy, you don't have as much time for friends, so you need to make sure that the few hours a month you can allocate to friends are well spent.

> *"I will not let anyone walk through my mind with their dirty feet."*

One of my favorite stories in our whole library is by Georgia Shaffer, who is an author, life coach, inspirational speaker, licensed psychologist, and cancer survivor. She wrote a story for the book that we made with Dr. Julie Silver of Harvard Medical School called *Chicken Soup for the Soul: Hope & Healing for Your Breast Cancer Journey.* I found this book so inspirational, because the stories in it transcend breast cancer, and are filled with useful life lessons for all of us. As I said in Chapter 18, the one about using the guest soap, cancer has a way of clarifying our thoughts, of cutting through the noise and letting us focus. And that's what Georgia did, as she shares in her story, "Eliminate the Negative, Accentuate the Positive."

Georgia wrote about what happened when she had a recurrence of her breast cancer. After the doctor gave her the bad news, his nurse, Vickie, held Georgia while she cried. She listened, she handed Georgia one tissue after another, and she stayed with her, supporting her, as long as she needed. Georgia says that having cancer taught her "the powerful impact of one caring person. Whether that person is a doctor's assistant like Vickie, a counselor, a friend or a relative — it's one person who can make a positive difference."

But Georgia had the opposite experience as well, and therein lay the lesson for me. A friend drove her to chemo one day but spent the entire fifty-minute drive relating "one painful story after another about people who had faced cancer."

"After previous treatments, I had never gotten sick," says Georgia. "After that treatment, I was sick for two days."

That led to her epiphany: "The harsh reality is that I became painfully aware that some people are not positive and life giving. Rather, their negative or thoughtless interactions are draining and, in some cases, toxic."

She goes on to say: "I learned the hard way that I needed to protect myself as much as possible from contact with that kind of negative or thoughtless person. At the very least I had to distance myself from certain people and acquire the ability to say no. This was especially difficult because I had been taught to be kind to everyone. I had never recognized the importance of setting clear boundaries with some people."

And here comes the part of Georgia's wisdom that hit me hard: "I had never realized that just like the weeds in a garden rob the flowers of vital moisture, nutrients and sunlight, so too the 'weeds' in my life were robbing me of the vital energy I needed to fight cancer and heal. I could not afford to allow interactions with negative people to steal the few resources I had left."

It would take time to make her cancer go away, slowly and painfully, but Georgia could make that toxic friend go away right then and there!

This is fabulous advice. We absolutely should weed the gardens of our lives on a regular basis, pulling out the negative so that everything else can thrive! I talked about using the Power of No for de-cluttering your calendar and your home in the previous chapter. But de-cluttering the people side of your life is imperative too. I let go of that frenemy, even though it makes me sad when I think of all the good times we had.

There's a great quote from Mahatma Gandhi that sums this up beautifully: "I will not let anyone walk through my mind with their dirty feet."

Georgia's story opened my eyes to the fact that I have a *right* to manage the friend side of my life. No more dirty feet walking through my mind.

We get to decide who our friends are. That sounds obvious, right? But is it? Think about it. How many friends do you have who don't add value to your life? You might find that you are reducing the time you spend with them and viewing your get-togethers as obligations instead of relaxing, fun breaks. You might be saying, "I have this friend… and I have to call her… she's always complaining… I don't like talking to her… but I have to."

Why? Why do you have to?

It's different if it's a family member. If they're family members, you love them and you spend time with them even if they drive you crazy. But friends are optional. You *get* to pick and choose. And *beyond* friends, you can *fire* doctors you don't like, workmen in your home you don't like, or anyone else in your world who is making you unhappy. There's almost always someone you might prefer who can do the same job.

***

The trick is identifying the toxic people in your life before you spend decades being "polluted" by them. Like me, Noelle Sterne didn't realize for a long time that she'd outgrown one friend's negativity until she finally paid attention to the nagging feeling she'd get after their monthly lunch dates. Meeting up with her toxic friend actually made Noelle *sick*.

In her story, "Time to Say Goodbye," which we published in *Chicken Soup for the Soul: Just Us Girls*, Noelle says that after one such lunch, she couldn't figure out why she felt so awful until she actually wrote down what happened in their time together, step by step, and saw it in black and white. The friend had complained about everything — from the traffic that morning, to how the restaurant napkins were folded, to how other friends raised their kids.

She lived in "a state of chronic indignation" and outrage, according to Noelle, and everything she saw was "cause for her righteous anger... Shopping on the Internet revealed the stupidity of retailers. Restaurant pasta less than *al dente* was a sin punishable by leaving the waiter two quarters. The supermarket checkers' sluggishness proved the regression of human evolution and threatened our entire civilization."

Now, I look forward to seeing 100% of my friends!

After a few hours of it, Noelle would absorb the anger and get a headache. In the past, she realized, "Sometimes I'd sympathized with her constant diatribes and even joined in." But now she was done with that. She looked at the long list of complaints her friend spat out and "the truths scribbled out in my journal couldn't be denied," says Noelle.

Like a love affair gone bad, Noelle understood that "it was time to say goodbye."

***

I have finally gotten to the point, after several years of "weeding," where I do not have toxic people in my life. Every single one of them is gone! What a relief.

Now, I look forward to seeing 100% of my friends! And I also smile at the workmen who come to the house because I like them and trust them. I like everyone at work as people, not just as colleagues, and feel like I'm spending the day with friends when I'm at the office.

And now that my friends are 100% non-toxic and add value to my life, I work hard to squeeze them into my ridiculously busy schedule, which is not only filled with work, and four grown kids who must be visited in their far-flung locations, and elderly parents, but also with marriage and duties at home and in my community.

But it's so important to make that time for friends. Today, when I was supposed to be writing this portion of the book, I stole away to have a two-hour lunch with friends. It's healthy to get out in the "real world" occasionally, a place where people know you as an individual separately from your kids or your job or even your spouse.

Sometimes I think that I should make a checklist of my friends and make sure that I have lunch with one of them every week until I get through the list—just schedule it and make it happen. After all, it would only be two hours a week.

We always talk about how you have to make time for exercise—you know, "do something for yourself" every day. But I think that making time for friends may be equally good for us. It recharges us, takes us away from our normal responsibilities for a short time, and reminds us that we are more than a parent, a spouse, a lawyer, a cashier, an editor, or whatever else we are called.

The Greek playwright Euripides said, "It is a good thing to be rich, and it is a good thing to be strong, but it is a better thing to be loved of many friends." So I guess he agreed—work is a good thing; staying strong through fitness is good; but the best thing is to have friends.

I get a lot of good advice from the people who write for us, and another story that made a big impression on me was "Mom's Night Out" by Mimi Greenwood Knight, which we published in *Chicken Soup for the Soul: Parenthood*. Mimi writes about how much she looks forward to her night out with friends each month, saying, "Nothing can bother me today—not the mud tracked all over the carpet, not the half-hour search for my car keys, not the eternity spent on hold with the insurance company, not the crayon on the living room wall. Tonight is the night when my friends and I leave the kids at home and get to act like kids ourselves."

Mimi writes about the "support, encouragement, and friendship" she gets on her night out and how "therapeutic" it is. Afterwards, she says, "I have renewed energy and my positive outlook is back. I feel like I can take on the world."

That is what a friend, not a frenemy, does for us... and how we can tell the difference between the two.

I felt just like that as I drove back to my computer today, like I had been on a mini-vacation. I returned to my writing recharged and enthusiastic. All that from a two-hour lunch with friends!

It's a simple truth. Friends make us feel good about ourselves and the world around us, while frenemies do the opposite.

Friend, frenemy, foe or rival; it doesn't matter what you call them. What matters is identifying who they are and deciding for yourself once and for all that you have the right to not waste one more precious minute with the wrong people.

It's Not About You

Grumpy cashier? Surly teenager? Mean boss? Don't take it personally!

You've decided to remove toxic people from your life, but you still need to deal with the people who are part of your everyday experience whether you like it or not. And this ties back to Chapter 14, in which I explained why I would be the world's worst therapist. Why? Because I would just smile and softly say, "It's Not About You."

That's right. If it's not about you, then there's no reason to take it personally. And if you don't take it personally, everything becomes so much easier to handle. And there's no need to get angry about it.

"Don't take it personally" is the single best piece of advice I give other mothers as they navigate their children's teen years. I've shared this advice with friends and with strangers. I remember explaining this to a mother on a chairlift one day, during the ten minutes that we spent together soaring over the ski slopes. She was so grateful. She said this changed everything for her!

It worked for me. My kids' teen years were fairly easy, but it wasn't because they were that much better behaved than other kids. They got good grades and were on varsity sports teams, but they also engaged in some of the normal undesirable high school behavior, usually involving beer.

Luckily I didn't learn about most of it till years later, more so with Ella than with Mike, who got caught more easily. Girls are so much better about hiding the evidence. Or maybe moms are just naïve. One time when I saw bags of empty beer cans in the trunk of Ella's car I actually believed her sports team was collecting them for fundraising purposes — you know, to get the nickel per can. Boys are easier — their friends post the party photos on Facebook. Or they forget and leave one stray, sticky ping-pong ball in a corner of your suspiciously clean kitchen when you come home from a business trip… and you don't have a ping-pong table.

What made the teenage years pleasant for me was that I knew the kids' behavior wasn't directed at me; it was just something that teens do. They can be really dumb! As I would affectionately tell my teenage son when I was explaining why he had a curfew: "You lack wisdom, judgment, and common sense."

> "Don't take it personally" is the single best piece of advice I give other mothers as they navigate their children's teen years.

I remember when one of my friends picked up her teenage daughter at school one beautiful spring afternoon and was reprimanded for not opening her convertible, turning on the radio, and enjoying the nice weather. The next day my friend picked up her daughter again, this time as directed: with the top down and music playing. Her daughter said she was embarrassing. My friend and I laughed about it and recalled how we treated our own mothers when we were teenagers.

Some of my friends took it personally when their teens were rude or got in trouble. They would say things like "I can't believe he did that to me." Did they really think their kids were doing those things *to them*? I doubt those kids thought about their parents for one second while they were playing beer pong with their friends.

If all else fails, remember what the columnist Doug Larson said: "Few things are more satisfying than seeing your children have teenagers of their own." But more about revenge later in this chapter!

My attitude has *always* been that it's not about me. I had a lot of surgery as a child and as a young woman — major surgeries adding up to multiple weeks in the hospital over many years — and yet I never let it get to me. Sure it stunk that I missed most of day camp the summer that I was eight years old, but these things happen. I don't remember feeling sorry for myself. I do remember, however, that there was a mean nurse who forced me to eat a cream cheese and jelly sandwich, which was disgusting. It's funny that sandwich is the biggest trauma I remember suffering as an eight-year-old who was stuck in the hospital for more than two weeks.

If anything, going through all those hospitalizations when I was young made me a better adult: tougher, more resilient, more understanding of hardship, and more certain that there can be a positive outcome even when things seem to be darkest.

When bad things happen to me, my attitude is *so what?* It's not like the universe is out to get *me*. Stuff happens to people.

That also applies when bad things happen in the form of personal interactions.

When I encounter someone rude, or someone who seems truly angry — a stranger, such as someone working at a store — I remind myself that he or she is not being rude to me specifically. Maybe she hates her job, or maybe he is worried about something in his family, or maybe the customer right before me was difficult. But I remind myself that I'm not important to that person. That person certainly doesn't care enough about *me* to manufacture that rudeness for *me*. *It's not about me.*

This applies to people you *do* know as well. Sometimes you're just a convenient victim for them, a way for them to express their misery. There is something called an anger triangle. That's when someone lashes out at you because you are an easier, safer target than the person he or she is truly mad at.

I remember last year I was having trouble with a business associate who was going through major personal problems. He started lashing out at me even though we had been friends and had a wonderful business relationship for six years.

One Sunday he called me at home and started screaming. My husband couldn't believe that I sat there calmly listening to my cell phone as this guy screamed. I let him scream for twenty minutes, holding the phone away from my ear. My husband said, "Why don't you hang up?" I told him that I didn't mind listening and that I might learn something.

It didn't bother me. I knew that this poor guy was in distress and I happened to be someone very important to him in a world that was falling apart. A few hours later, he called me again, quiet and friendly, asking me for help because his wife was so concerned about his mental state that she had forced him to check into a hospital.

I don't understand why anyone would take it personally when someone is obviously reacting to his or her own issues. I can think of many times in my life when someone has yelled at me and I've stood there and looked at the person and analyzed the situation.

One time, I stood in a conference room, in front of dozens of traders at a brokerage firm, while the head trader, Louie, yelled at me about a stock that had gone down. The firm had hired me as an outside consultant to educate them about the telecommunications industry and help them take a company public — an IPO. The stock had done well for a while and then something had gone wrong and the stock fell. So Louie, this stocky little guy, was yelling at *me*... because he was afraid to yell at his own bosses, the ones who had made the decision to do the IPO.

It was pretty cowardly really, yelling at this 5'3" woman who was just a consultant. But even then, and this was when I was only in my early thirties, I didn't let it get to me. I knew he wasn't really mad *at me*. He was angry about the situation and he was a seriously flawed person who decided to vent by yelling at a girl in front of dozens of men. The whole time he was yelling at me, I was *redefining* him (Chapter 16). He reminded me of the tailor my family went to throughout my childhood to get dresses and pants hemmed. While he yelled, I had a mental image of him kneeling at my feet with pins in his mouth, mumbling, "So how short do you want it?" Maybe I'm weird but that worked very well for me!

The fact is that getting angry is a waste of time — especially because, as you already know, *it's not about you.* I don't know its origin, but there is a great quote that goes something like this: "For every minute you are angry, you lose sixty seconds of happiness."

Getting angry would make me feel bad, and there's no reason to get angry if I don't take it personally, so I try to keep those feelings under control. I'm not a saint though. Here's what I tell myself when I am confronted by a real jerk like that guy Louie: "He is stuck with being himself." That is the best revenge, isn't it? I am not that unhappy, unpleasant person. I get to be *me*, not *him*.

> "He who angers you conquers you."

The Australian nurse Elizabeth Kenny said it best: "He who angers you conquers you." If you react to that rude person, and you become unhappy too, you have let him win. And you will then transfer that unhappiness to someone else.

Several years after Louie yelled at me, believe it or not, I was offered the position of Vice Chairman of his firm! A friend of mine was considering buying that brokerage firm and he thought that adding me to the team would help them establish credibility and bring in clients. I told him that the only reason I would take the job was so that I could fire Louie — you know that old saying: "the best revenge is served cold." But of course I didn't take the job. It was nice to know that it was an option, though!

I tried to instill anger management skills in my kids as they were growing up. My kids are great friends and always have been. But when they were little they fought a lot, which is normal for kids who are two years apart. Some of the fights were pretty funny.

I'd hear excuses like, "Well, *she* hit me *second*." And when I'd send Mike to his room as punishment for hitting Ella, she'd trot off with him to continue playing even though she was the one who wanted him to be punished.

I had a rule when the kids were arguing about something. They each had to stand on a piece of furniture if they wanted to keep fighting. So there they were — Mike on one chair, Ella on another — and they would inevitably burst out laughing at how silly they looked and the argument would die a natural death.

The kids are grown now, so as an empty nester I get to practice my anger management theories on Bill instead. Lucky him! Since it drives me crazy when he complains about the other drivers on the road, we have a new rule. Every time he wants to complain about another driver he has to say something nice about that person instead. After all, they're not driving badly to purposely irk him or ruin *his* day. It's not about him, so there's no reason to get angry.

Bill has resorted to blowing kisses at the offending drivers. It's funny to watch him exclaim, "I love you, Dodge Caravan Minivan Driver from New Jersey," and then blow kisses in the minivan's direction. But it redirects his emotions and we laugh instead of getting steamed up.

Once you realize that all the crummy things going on around you aren't *for* you, *about* you, *because* of you, or in *spite* of you, your stress level will plummet. With enough practice, not only will you emotionally detach from other people's undesirable behavior, but you may even be able to turn your response — and theirs — around and have a good laugh.

As Alan Alda said, "When people are laughing, they're generally not killing each other."

Reduce Stress
with Six Easy Tips

Even if you are into extreme
multitasking, these work

Y ou're going to eliminate the toxic people from your life and you've learned not to take it personally when someone is nasty to you, but you're still going to have stress. I understand that. Here are six easy tips to help you handle it.

These tips work, and they don't require anything more from you than a change of attitude. That's what I like — tips that don't require you to make big changes or attend a seminar or write letters to yourself or do anything that will only add to your to-do list and thus your *stress*! I like tips that you can accomplish in *one second* merely by telling yourself to think differently.

So here we go:

Tip 1. Remember to use your positive thinking.

Let's say you need to do some errands at the mall and you have to park a quarter mile away at the farthest end of the parking lot. There is absolutely a silver lining. You can say to yourself, *Oh good. I didn't have time to exercise today but now I'm forced to do what I meant to do anyway. I get to take a little walk.*

Making a conscious effort to find the positives in your life, to find the silver linings even in the everyday hassles, will make you feel better. There's always a silver lining or a way to redefine something.

Tip 2. Count your blessings.

You're busy because you have a lot of things going on... because your life is interesting and filled with people you care about and things you care about doing. I know that I am usually overwhelmed by how much work I have to do, and then I add on more, in the form of having people over for dinner or cleaning out a closet to donate stuff to the thrift shop... or taking on the commitment of writing and recording a podcast five days a week when I should be working on this book!

Instead of focusing on how much you have to do, think about *why* you have all those things to do. You *love* what you're doing—whether it's a job or volunteer work or being a domestic goddess for your favorite people in the whole world—your family.

Gratitude and thankfulness are scientifically proven to make people healthier and more popular. Remember that the reason you have so much to do is that you live a *wondrous* and *full* life.

Tip 3. Say "no."

You can do it. If you don't want to bake five-dozen cookies for an event next week, say "no." If your full and wondrous life is as full and wondrous as you can handle, then say "no" to that new task that's being asked of you. I routinely say "no" when my husband asks me to do something extra at home or at the office. I tell him that my head will explode and he backs off.

Tip 4. Don't strive for absolute perfection.

It doesn't have to be perfect. I talk about that a lot because I've learned to be a realist. I want our books to be perfect, but at some point I have to stop editing them, push the Send button, and get those files off to the printer.

I'm the same way at home. I love to entertain and we throw together lots of last-minute dinner parties. I won't obsess over every part of the dinner, and I'm happy to order take-out if that's what it takes to pull it off. The key is who's sitting *around* the table, not what's *on* the table. If I had to make it perfect, I wouldn't do it, and then we wouldn't see our friends.

Tip 5. Take care of yourself.

Busy people need to look out for themselves. I'm not saying I'm great at this, but I try. And while I don't always take care of myself physically, i.e. get in my daily walks, the one thing that I'm adamant about is reading before I go to bed. I make a big point of stopping my work by ten so that I can start slowing down for bed. And no matter how late I get in bed, even if we've been out at a party, I read before I go to sleep. I'll use a Kindle or my phone to read an e-book so as not to bother my husband.

Tip 6. Carve your to-do list into tiny pieces.

This always works for me. Look at the trees, not the forest. In other words, don't think about the whole, huge task in front of you. Break it into little do-able pieces and deal with them a little bit at a time. Do not look at the whole gigantic mess of a to-do list that you have. Bill loves it when I break down his tasks at home this way, for example, before one of those last-minute dinner parties. I write his tasks — turn on outdoor lights, make ice, load CDs into the stereo, and open wine — on little Post-it notes, one task per yellow slip of paper, and he's a happy husband.

And while you're at it, why not delete a few items from your list? After all, everything doesn't have to be perfect, and you have the right to say "no."

***

I want to share a few helpful stories with you as well, from a very cool book that was coauthored by Dr. Jeff Brown of Harvard Medical School with health writer Liz Neporent. It's called *Chicken Soup for the Soul: Say Goodbye to Stress* and it was one of several innovative books that we made a few years ago with professors from Harvard Medical School. So these are doctor-approved stories that will help you reduce stress!

The first story is called "It's Not the End of the World," and it's by one of our regular writers, April Knight. April tells us that she was always nervous, even as a child. She would break out in hives over things other children seemed to take in stride.

April was desperately anxious to please people and she was very critical of herself when something went wrong. When she was five and about to play in a piano recital, she got violently ill on the stage. And a few years later, during a school play, she got so nervous that she walked off the stage and took a nosedive into the audience.

April started avoiding any situation where she might fail, even normal social events. She worried that she would say the wrong thing, spill something, or make a fool of herself in some other way.

Of course, avoiding the world didn't actually solve any problems for April. It just turned her into a *lonely* person who still worried about everything.

> **"Worry is a misuse of imagination."**

Then, one day, April was walking to the store when she tripped over the curb and fell on her knee. An elderly man came to her aid, helped her up, and asked if she was hurt.

Once he knew she was okay, he said something that changed April's life: "Well, if you didn't break your knees, then it isn't the end of the world, is it? There's no reason to be embarrassed. We all fall down sometimes. You're okay now."

Suddenly everything was put in perspective for her. It wasn't the end of the world. *Nothing* that had ever happened to her was the end of the world.

You may not feel this is relevant to you, if you're not a world-class worrier like April was. But if you're like me, and you worry about more normal things, like how you're going to get all your work done, or what might go wrong on your vacation, or whether you are prepared for that meeting that's coming up, then April's next epiphany is for you.

April realized that virtually *all the things* she was worrying about *hadn't happened yet.* They were all future possibilities, not even future *probabilities*, just *possibilities.*

That led April to do something really smart — something useful, do-able, and easy. She began writing down the things that were troubling her the most: debts, family problems, the funny noise under the hood of her car. No matter how big or how small the problem was, she'd write it on a piece of paper and put the piece of paper in a box.

On the last day of the month she'd open the box and read the list of problems she had anticipated *might* happen. April learned that most of those problems never became a reality, and if they did, they weren't a big deal.

Over time, April found herself putting fewer and fewer notes into her "worry box," and some months the box stays empty. She still has the same thoughts about what might go wrong, but now she puts those worries in perspective. They're not that big a deal. And as that wise old man pointed out, they're not the end of the world.

I love this quote from bestselling author Dan Zadra, who knows a thing or two about getting a lot done in a short period of time: "Worry is a misuse of imagination." That's probably why he's successful — he funnels all his energy into being creative and imagining what could go right, not spending his time on worrying.

***

Here's another stress-relieving tip from that same book. This story is near and dear to my heart because it's basically about flipping the conventional wisdom over, and as I said in Tip 6, looking at the trees, not the forest.

I know that contravenes the accepted wisdom, but I avoid looking at the forest. I look at the trees. You know that old saying: "He can't see the forest for the trees." I look at the forest when I start a project, but I quickly switch to the trees. If I looked at the forest in this job, publishing a book a month, plus recording five podcasts a week, plus doing all the other things I do, I would go insane. The only way I get through each day is conquering the task one tree at a time.

My survival strategy is to turn everything I have to do into tiny bite-size pieces. And I've used that strategy with my kids too. When my seventeen-year-old son was completely overwhelmed by college applications, I turned the process into a very *long* list of very *short* projects, which got him unstuck.

A very wise mom named Marilyn Turk did the same thing for her son, as she tells us in her story called "Bite by Bite." Her teenage son Bret was completely overwhelmed. He had always been a good student, jovial and carefree. He got good grades and he handled the workload.

> *I look at the forest when I start a project, but I quickly switch to the trees.*

But you know what happens as high school goes on. By junior year the kids are under tremendous pressure. They know that their grades matter now, they're studying for the SAT or ACT, they may be working part-time or doing a sport that takes hours a day. And then there's still romance and friends to fit in. Plus they need a lot of sleep because they're still growing.

On the day in question, Marilyn had never seen Bret so upset. He plopped down in a chair, pulled out some papers and showed Marilyn what he had to do: a project for the Science Fair for his chemistry teacher; an algebra test that would be one-third of the grade for the semester (and Bret hated algebra); an essay for English composition; and studying for midterms, which were coming the next week! Plus, Bret needed help with Spanish.

Marilyn felt so bad for her son. His hands were shaking and he was on the verge of tears. We've all had times when we felt it was completely impossible to do what needed to be done. Marilyn had been through this herself at her company, where she was a sales manager. She was always trying to please upper management by producing results from her sales team but then she also had to deal with her ten salespeople, who were worried about making their quotas while still taking care of their customers properly.

It got particularly bad for Marilyn when she had to do all that, plus plan the company's sales meeting. She was in charge of the agenda, setting up the presentations, arranging the people who would participate, ordering supplies, and so on.

Marilyn had learned to put every single part of the task on a list, along with a deadline for each item. Then she put all the items in order. This might seem obvious to those of us who have done this a lot, but it was a revelation to Bret.

Marilyn looked at him and said, "You don't have to do everything at once. You can do one at a time. Let's make a list of what you need to do."

Together, they made the list and put the due date next to each item. They even listed who could help him with each project and what supplies he would need. Marilyn watched Bret visibly relax as they made the list.

From that day on, Bret made lists for everything he had to do. Marilyn found lists on pieces of paper all over the house. She finishes her story by quoting that adage that asks, "How do you eat an elephant?" The answer: "One bite at a time."

Sometimes, even though that whole list-making process seems obvious, the best thing you can do for people who are feeling overwhelmed and panic-stricken is to help them organize their thoughts into a list. And when it's you, and you are so frenzied that you can't even make the list for yourself, ask someone to help you.

That's what I did with Natasha Stoynoff, who has been advising me through the process of creating this book — acting as writing coach, editor, and cheerleader. She sat me down and helped me come up with the table of contents. Believe it or not, that took three full days, but it was a great way to organize "the forest" and turn it into a lot of little ten-page "trees" that I could chop down.

***

Now here's your third story from *Say Goodbye to Stress*. It's called

"All You Can Do," and in it, Beth Arvin presents an idea that I haven't seen before in any other Chicken Soup for the Soul story. This is going to turn into my seventh stress-busting tip!

The story starts with Beth saying, "I'm sorry, that's all the money I can send right now. I will pay more when I can," to a debt collector on the phone. Then Beth hangs up and breaks down in tears.

Three months earlier, when Beth was stopped in traffic, a young woman drove into the back of her car. Beth was pushed forward into the steering wheel, and she suffered two badly sprained ankles, a very swollen knee, some spinal injuries and a concussion that left her mind cloudy for weeks.

Beth was self-employed in a job that required physical strength and being on her feet, so she was unable to work for a while. She was a single mother with a child in college, and she had no safety net, no disability insurance, and no employer who would carry her. She would get some kind of financial settlement from the accident eventually, but that would take a long time and it wouldn't pay her immediate bills. She still had to pay rent and utilities and her daughter's tuition and her credit card bill.

This was not an irresponsible person who was living large. Beth was just experiencing a cash flow problem while she waited for the settlement. I know in my own case, after I was rear-ended in my car and suffered a major injury and loss of income, it took a couple of years before I got the settlement from the other driver's insurance company even though they said right from the start that they were responsible.

Poor Beth was struggling financially, emotionally, and also, physically, from the spinal injury.

"At times my body would seize in spasms," she said, "but the tears that fell came more from worry than pain. My mind was filled with fear. My blood pressure had risen dangerously."

Then things got worse.

Her older sister was diagnosed with cancer and did not have

long to live.

Beth was crushed. She prayed to God and asked how she was supposed to bear this on top of everything else. The answer she heard was this: "Have you done your best?"

She thought about it. Yes, she decided, she was doing her best. She was working as many hours as she could handle despite her injuries. She had cut her spending as much as possible. She was diligent about her physical therapy. And she was supporting and comforting her sister, which was all she could do for her.

Once Beth had her answer, that she was doing her best, everything changed for her. She was at peace. There was nothing more she could do.

And that was the solution, one that I really like. If you are doing everything that you can, you deserve to be at peace.

As soon as Beth had that new peace, the phone rang again. It was the credit card debt collector. They had been calling once or twice a week, always asking the same questions, getting the same answers, then giving Beth the same lecture on the importance of meeting her obligations.

This time, Beth changed her answer. She said, "I'm sorry, but there is no change in my circumstances. I'm not sure when I can get current. I know you are just doing your job, but I can't do anything more than what I am doing and the stress has been affecting my physical wellbeing. I'm not trying to be evasive. As soon as I can I will get current. In the meantime, I just can't let this ruin my health. I'm not willing to have a heart attack wondering when I can pay you."

There was silence on the line. Then Beth heard the woman say, "Good for you. It's not worth dying for. Of course, I'm still going to have to keep making these calls." Somehow that exchange was a lot less stressful for Beth. She took the deepest breath she had in months.

Beth's sister did pass away twelve weeks after her diagnosis.

And Beth continued to suffer financial problems and some pain from the car accident. But she had a new approach. She asked herself whether she was doing the best that she could, and when the answer was yes, as it often was, she remained at peace with her circumstances.

* * *

For some of us, these stress-busting tips might be the most important part of the whole book, because stress can *paralyze* us. It has happened to me many times, but I have gotten so much better at dealing with it by implementing my six, *now seven*, tips:

1) Use my positive thinking to redefine the circumstances;

2) Count my blessings and remember the joyful reasons that put me in this position of having so much to do;

3) Say "no" and slim down my to-do list;

4) Remember it doesn't have to be perfect;

5) Take care of myself no matter how busy I am;

6) Focus on the "trees" not the whole, big, scary "forest."

And now, thanks to Beth Arvin,

7) Give myself credit for doing the best that I can do. Once I've done the best that I can do, I can relax. There's nothing more to be done than that.

Change Your Life in One Second

Forgiveness is powerful — it can set you free

Before I wrap up this crash course in Chicken Soup for the Soul advice and wisdom, I want to cover one of the most important lessons I've learned from all our stories: the power of forgiveness. Basically, without forgiveness — of other people and of *yourself* — you're stuck. It's hard to make other improvements in your life or find true happiness if you're harboring resentment and stewing about something.

Let's start with *self*-forgiveness. When I began my research for *Chicken Soup for the Soul: The Power of Forgiveness*, I spoke to the well-known psychotherapist Dr. Robi Ludwig, who stressed how important it was to include stories about self-forgiveness. I was grateful for her advice.

Many of us are quick to forgive other people but we are hard on ourselves. I've always thought there was something rather illogical about excusing other people's transgressions but holding *yourself* to a higher standard and deeming *yourself* unworthy of forgiveness. If you haven't forgiven yourself for whatever you did wrong or whatever you *think* you did wrong, you may find yourself unable to move forward in your life and have meaningful relationships. Therefore, I think it's important to give yourself the same benefit of the doubt that you would give to someone else.

This is related to that last story in Chapter 22, the one about how Beth Arvin found peace with her financial problems once she accepted that she was doing the best she could. If you did the best that you could, but you failed, why *wouldn't* you forgive yourself? And once you accepted that you had done the best you could, so that you were worthy of forgiveness, why wouldn't you *extend* that same forgiveness to *someone else* who also did the best that he or she could?

We had a wonderful story about this in *Chicken Soup for the Soul: The Power of Forgiveness.* Imagine this scene: The front door slams. Judythe Guarnera opens it and sees her husband of almost thirty years tromping across the front lawn. He looks back at her in the doorway and quietly says, "You're wrong, you know. There was never anyone else but you. No one. Ever."

> It's hard to make other improvements in your life or find true happiness if you're harboring resentment.

With these words, he disappears into his car, and Judythe stands there, reassured that he is not having an affair but still facing the end of her marriage.

Judythe starts crying and thinking about the early years of their marriage and how in love they were. They built a life together, going through all those start-up years — you know, the ones when you scrape the money together to buy a house, have those little kids, and live simply. It's a joint effort and you do it together.

Then, somehow, Judythe and her husband started to grow apart. When they became empty nesters, she finally got to finish her college degree, something that was personally fulfilling but didn't seem to change the negative path their marriage was on.

Judythe says they were very different people. She was outgoing and not afraid to share her opinions. Her husband was quieter and more introspective.

When they eventually decided to get a divorce, it was acrimonious. They battled endlessly and said a lot of things to each other that could never be taken back.

Judythe joined a divorce support group but she was still stuck — she hadn't found a good way to shed all her resentment and anger and move forward. Then a wonderful, insightful speaker addressed the group and said, "Repeat after me. In my marriage I did the best I could."

Everyone in the room said it. Then, the speaker told them to say, "My spouse did the best he or she could."

Now there was silence. No one was willing to say that! The speaker started to persuade them, saying, "Who would choose to do their worst?"

And she was right. I think if most of us think back to whatever relationships have failed for us — a marriage, a friendship, a work situation — we know that we did our best. So why can't we assume that the other people also did their best? They might not have done a good job, but if they were *trying*, it's a lot harder to be angry.

Judythe thought about this a lot, and she realized that her husband probably *had* done his best, just as she had. She says, "It took a while before I could embrace that idea and forgive my husband and myself. He wasn't the best husband for me and I wasn't the best wife for him. But I had loved him and had really intended to do my best." She said that when she thought about her own past she saw that it was indeed made up of all her best efforts.

And so was her husband's. That's why Judythe's story is called "We Did Our Best."

There is a Chinese proverb that says, "Gold cannot be pure, and people cannot be perfect." When we learn to reevaluate our own behavior in light of our own imperfections, we become less judgmental of others as well.

***

Self-forgiveness is imperative, but you'll probably find that what you make use of more often is the skill of forgiving others. Jean Morris described an interesting approach in her story, "The List," in *Chicken Soup for the Soul: Time to Thrive.* Jean's husband Greg had announced that he wanted a divorce after more than thirty years of marriage, three children, and four grandchildren. He said the marriage had "lost its spark" and he wanted a chance to find his "soul mate."

They didn't fight over the possessions. He offered to let Jean stay in the spacious 1840s-era farmhouse they'd lovingly restored and said he wanted to split everything 50/50. Jean didn't want to stay, though. It was time to make a fresh start. She found a small contemporary house and got ready to move.

Then she began the overwhelming task of deciding what to take with her. Some decisions were easy. She'd leave her husband's ugly brown recliner and take her great-grandmother's oak dining table. She'd leave the dishes adorned with moose and elk and grizzly bears for her husband, but she would take the wedding china. She'd take the treadmill and give him the pool table.

Jean and Greg continued to split everything harmoniously. They even split the pets, with Jean keeping the dog and Greg taking the cat.

It was easy, and before she knew it Jean was spending her first night in her new house. But now she was in tears. She thought about all the decisions she had made — what to take and what to leave — and she realized she hadn't done the *hard* work yet.

She clicked on her bedside lamp and got to work with pen and paper. Jean explains the very powerful discovery that she made next:

"At the top of a blank page, I wrote WHAT TO LEAVE BEHIND. The list wasn't long, but it was powerful. Anger. Resentment. Hurt. Desire for revenge. Fear, the most overwhelming emotion of all. Fear that I wasn't brave enough or smart enough or tough enough to weather this gigantic storm.

"Atop the next page, I wrote WHAT TO KEEP. Try as I might, I could come up with only one item to put on the list: Happy Memories. Memories of bringing our newborn babies home from the hospital. Of the smell of wood smoke and fresh-cut Christmas trees. Of throwing hay from the barn loft to the horses waiting eagerly below. Of bicycle rides and basketball games and BB-shooting contests. Of tire swings and trampolines. Of fishing in the pond and catching nothing but snapping turtles. Of snuggling in front of the TV with a huge bowl of popcorn to share. Of Easter dresses and prom dresses and wedding dresses.

> *"Never does the human soul appear so strong as when it foregoes revenge and dares to forgive an injury."*

"I filled page after page of that notebook with happy memories. By the time my fingers grew too stiff to grasp the pen, the sky outside my bedroom window was growing pink."

That was what Jean needed. She *shed her resentment, banished her fear,* and *redefined her past by focusing on all the good.* She focused on all the good things that had happened and forgave the bad, so that the bad things wouldn't hold her back. And then she watched the first sunrise of her new life, filled with excitement and ready for adventure.

***

What I love about forgiveness is that it gives you the opportunity to change your life literally in one second. All you have to do is *decide* that you're going to do it. It's like raising your shoulders and shrugging off a heavy cloak that is weighing you down. It requires no time, no money, no sweating… you don't even need to talk to anyone! Even the person you are forgiving doesn't have to know. You just shrug off that heavy cloak, let it fall to the ground, and move forward, feeling light and free.

Forgiveness is a gift that you give to *yourself*. I was astounded by how many of our writers talked about the freedom they felt after forgiving someone. They hadn't realized how much they were harming themselves by holding onto resentment. Often the person they were mad at didn't even know, so that person — the "bad" person — was blissfully getting on with life, while the "injured" person was the only one who was suffering.

Joe Rector wrote a story for our forgiveness book called "Coaching the Coach" about what happened when he resigned as coach of his son's baseball team. He couldn't take the complaining anymore from the parents who said their sons weren't getting enough playing time. Joe and his co-coach had decided to rotate all twelve boys on the team so that they would get equal playing time regardless of ability.

The very last boy added to the roster happened to be an above-average player and his father in particular couldn't accept that his above-average son wasn't getting an above-average amount of playing time. When Joe quit, that father took his spot. And then he exacted revenge on Joe by benching his son for the next few games. When Joe confronted him, the new coach kicked Joe's son off the team altogether.

Joe says, "I held my tongue for a while, but eventually, the injustice of it all got to me. I couldn't believe that my son was kicked off a team I'd help to build." He goes on to say, "For the next couple of years, I couldn't even think of that other coach without becoming so angry that my blood pressure spiked. When I saw him at games throughout the coming seasons, I turned and walked away, refusing to speak to a man that I hated for the pain he'd inflicted on my son."

Joe remained angry for years, until one day his son said to him, "Dad, it's time to quit being mad. I'm okay now and don't care." Joe realized he was right and he forgave the other father. He says, "Almost immediately, I felt as if a huge weight had been lifted from my shoulders." And he was able to enjoy watching his son play baseball again. The only person Joe had been hurting during all those years was Joe.

***

That father really *was* trying to hurt Joe and his son. But often the offending party in your life didn't hurt you on purpose. One strategy is to focus on the motivation of the other person. If you come to believe that he or she didn't do it on purpose, all the resentment should disappear. We saw this a lot in stories about fathers who would lose touch with their children and then be uncertain what to do. Rather than reaching out to have a relationship with their children, they'd be afraid to try, and the years apart would add up.

Anthony Anderson, the actor and producer — and star of the ABC hit, *Black-ish* — was my coauthor for *Chicken Soup for the Soul: The Power of Forgiveness*. He shared his own story, "The Forgiveness of Robert and Me," about finally having a meaningful conversation with his mostly absentee biological father right before he died.

It took a diagnosis of liver cancer for Anthony's father Robert to really talk to his son. Anthony says that he visited Robert a few days before he died and they spent more than three hours together.

"We talked about everything, but most of all we talked about having a relationship," says Anthony. "We both agreed that it was finally time to bury the hatchet and move forward as father and son. He finally said five little words that I had been waiting a lifetime to hear: 'I'm sorry, I love you.' It moved me to tears. I repeated those words to him. We hugged and called it a night. I saw the joy in his eyes."

Now, Anthony says, "I sleep peacefully at night knowing that I was able to release my father from a burden of guilt as well as Robert releasing me from the burden of anger I had towards him."

"Our relationship was the last wrong that my father needed to right before passing on," he says. "I believe he held on just long enough to do so. That night I forgave him and he forgave me. We had wiped our slate clean and I was ready to start anew, but unfortunately we were out of time."

***

One of the most memorable forgiveness stories that we have is from Immaculée Ilibagiza, the author, with Steve Erwin, of *Left to Tell: Discovering God Amidst the Rwandan Holocaust*. Immaculée is well known as one of the survivors of the Rwandan genocide.

Rwanda was paradise, says Immaculée — breathtakingly beautiful, with "mist-shrouded mountains, lush green hills and sparkling lakes." It wasn't only the location, though. It was an idyllic place to grow up because of the friendly people. Everyone got along, despite the fact that there were two tribes in Rwanda — the majority Hutu and the minority Tutsi, of which she was a member. No one paid attention to the tribal differences; there was intermarriage, and there were blended families, friendships and working relationships without regard to tribal affiliation.

Then, when Immaculée was twenty-four years old, on April 7, 1994, the presidential plane was shot down and extremist Hutu politicians commanded that the seven million Hutus should kill as many of the one million Tutsis as they could.

The world watched in horror as former friends, neighbors, and even family members turned on each other. As soldiers surrounded their home, Immaculée's father urged her to run to the pastor's house, saying, "He is Hutu, but he is a good man and will hide you. Go, Immaculée... go *now!*"

She spent the next three months crammed into a four by three–foot bathroom with seven other Tutsi women. The pastor pushed a piece of furniture in front of the bathroom door to hide its existence. The terrified women had to stand all the time, packed together like sardines, listening to the screams of those being killed outside the house.

It's understandable that Immaculée's heart began to fill with hatred for the killers. She wanted to see them suffer and die. This was a new feeling for her. She had been raised to forgive, not to fantasize about revenge. Immaculée prayed to God to help her and she managed to view the killers differently, as people who had lost their way. It felt good to have moved beyond the hatred.

When the genocide was over, Immaculée and her fellow captives emerged from the tiny bathroom to learn the fate of their families and friends. Her entire family had been killed, except for her eldest brother who had been studying abroad. She learned the gory details: her father had been shot while trying to protect other Tutsi families; her mother had been hacked to death on the street when she left her hiding place to help a child; her youngest brother was herded into a stadium along with thousands of other Tutsis and slaughtered by machine gun; and her older brother was killed by friends of the family. They chopped his head open but she heard that before he died, he actually forgave them.

Several months later, Immaculée was invited to the jail to meet the man behind the murders of her mother and older brother. She found a sick old man in chains. She knew him! He had been a successful businessman in their community and she had played with his children. But he was a Hutu and he had participated in the genocide.

Immaculée describes what happened: "The jailor kicked him in the ribs yelling, 'Stand up, Hutu! Stand up you pig and tell this girl why you murdered her mother and butchered her brother!'" Immaculée took pity on the ruined man. She crouched down, looked him in the eye, and said, "I forgive you."

And then, she says, "I turned and walked out of that prison free of anger and hatred and I have lived as a free woman ever since."

And that's why Immaculée's story is titled "The Greatest Gift."

***

The American preacher Edwin Hubbell Chapin said, "Never does the human soul appear so strong as when it foregoes revenge and dares to forgive an injury." I talked about revenge in Chapter 21, and how I have personally foregone it. It's fun to think about it once in a while, but definitely not the healthy thing to actually *do*.

We concluded our forgiveness book with one of my favorite poems that we've ever published: "The Road Ahead," by the very talented Boston-based freelance writer Christina Galeone. I can't think of a better way to conclude this chapter than to share it with you.

The Road Ahead

Anger
Begets anger.
Rage

Rumbles forward,
Steamrolling
Good as well as bad
On the road ahead.
Forgiveness
Begets forgiveness.
Peace
Shines from above,
Nurturing
All that is precious
On the road ahead.

Sometimes You Can't Explain The Unexplainable

Divine intervention, guardian angels, ESP, intuition, and who knows

You had a good dose of The Unexplainable in Chapter 13, when I told you about Carolyn's deceased mother warning her about the blood clots in her lungs and Chris's deceased father coming to him in the middle of the night to explain how to fix the bulldozer. The stories open our minds and make us more aware that sometimes you just have to sit back and accept that weird things happen. It makes life more mysterious and wonderful at the same time.

Most of us know somebody who knows somebody who's had a real life experience that is so fantastical and uncanny, you can't believe it happened. Then when you realize the storyteller (and that might be *you*) isn't making it up, you look for the logical explanation for it and after racking your brain, can't find one. The only thing left to do after that is scratch your head, give in to it, and accept and embrace the fact that life gives us mysterious gifts and we won't always understand the where, why, or how of them.

Do these things happen because of divine intervention? Guardian angels? ESP? Intuition? Karma? Random coincidence? Who knows?

Our *Chicken Soup for the Soul* books on these topics are bestsellers because we mere mortals can't help but be drawn to the thrill of the unknown, marveling at how the universe works in mysterious ways. The stories give us hope, and proof, that good things *can* happen to us even when logic would say there is *no* hope. I find that reading this kind of story — and we get thousands of them every year — makes me a happier person, because I am more aware of the good things that can happen even when we can't explain why.

* * *

I'm going to start with a story I tell all the time because I love the mystery of it. It's from our book *Chicken Soup for the Soul: Touched by an Angel* and it's by Johanna Richardson. You decide after you hear this. How did this happen?

> *Sometimes your gut tells you something that you wouldn't glean from reviewing "the facts."*

Johanna was driving home from working late and she was exhausted. She had been at the office for sixteen hours and she had a long drive ahead of her. Suddenly, out of nowhere, she felt an overwhelming need to see her husband's grandmother, who was in her nineties and in a nursing home even farther away than Johanna's home.

It was way after visiting hours and Johanna wouldn't get there until after eleven, so she decided it was a ridiculous impulse and she wouldn't do it. But then, as she was about to take the exit ramp to go home, Johanna felt the urge even more strongly — she stayed on the highway and drove to the nursing home.

When Johanna got to Grandma's room, she found her sitting on the side of her bed, awake and perky, with the light on. Grandma was thrilled to see her visitor. Not one minute later, who showed up but Johanna's husband! He was a police detective and had also been working late.

He whispered to Johanna that he felt like an idiot but he'd felt an urgent need to visit Grandma and had left in the middle of his shift.

They had a nice visit, sitting close to each other and holding hands, reminiscing about happy memories.

Johanna and her husband left the nursing home in the wee hours of the morning, Johanna to go home, and her husband to go back to work and make up the hours he had missed. Grandma asked if they could stay longer, but they couldn't. They told her they loved her, kissed her goodbye, and said they would return the next day.

Shortly after Johanna got home, the phone rang. It was the nursing home. Grandma had died in her sleep.

Johanna and her husband were stunned and heartbroken, but so grateful they had listened to their inner voices, or their gut feelings, or ESP from Grandma, or whatever it was that compelled them both, independently, to visit her in the middle of the night, something they had never done before.

The late Dr. Joyce Brothers said, "Trust your hunches. Hunches are usually based on facts filed away just below the conscious level." Sometimes your gut tells you something that you wouldn't glean from reviewing "the facts."

***

Now here's a real spine-tingling story. I wouldn't have believed this except that it comes from a very reliable friend of mine, Jeanne Blandford, who works at Chicken Soup for the Soul. Jeanne used to work in the publishing department as one of our editors and she's a wonderful writer. But her first love has always been dogs and cats, and a number of our staff now have rescue cats or dogs thanks to Jeanne's work with a local shelter. She sure knows how to sell those abandoned pets, and that's why she moved over to what I call "the bark side," meaning that she left our editorial staff and went to work for our pet food business in marketing.

Jeanne was reluctant to even *tell* me this story because she knew it was so incredible, but I pried it out of her and we included it in *Chicken Soup for the Soul: Messages from Heaven*. The story is called "Heart Attack" and it's about a dream that Jeanne had when she was a college student.

Jeanne was very close to her grandparents, who lived in a first-floor apartment in the New York City apartment building they managed.

In her dream, Jeanne is woken by her grandfather, who tells her to get dressed, take her grandmother's hand, follow him out the front door of the building, and go back in through the outside door to the basement. When he opens the door to the basement, there is an awful smell emanating from it but they go in anyway. Jeanne's grandfather whispers to her to hide her grandmother under a stairwell and then follow him. He looks terrified as he tells his wife that Jeanne will be back to take care of her later.

At that point in the dream, a huge shadow appears behind Jeanne and her grandfather. He tells her to run. She runs, but she looks back and she sees the shadow has turned into a massive man who is stabbing her grandfather in the heart.

Jeanne woke from that dream, crying, and then realized, with relief, that it was just a nightmare. She went to school that day and was sitting in an afternoon class when she suddenly stood up and announced, "My grandfather just died." She *knew*. This was almost forty years ago by the way. No cell phones.

Jeanne drove home and got the expected news when she arrived. Her grandfather had died of a heart attack at the exact time she had stood up in class. He had worked outside that day, raking leaves, and then had given his wife a big kiss and laid down for a rest, arms crossed, as if he knew and he was assuming the position.

This was all strange enough, right? But it gets stranger.

A few months later, Jeanne's grandmother had a heart attack too, but she survived it. When Jeanne visited her in the hospital, her grandmother was visibly relieved to see her. By then, she was suffering from a bit of dementia, but what she said next was pretty spooky.

She pulled Jeanne close and whispered, "I thought you were dead. I thought he got you."

Jeanne asked, "*Who* got me?"

"That man. The man that killed your grandfather in the basement." Jeanne froze as her grandmother continued: "You saved me, Jeanne. You hid me under the staircase. I was so afraid but Pop said you would come back and you did. He said you would come back and take care of me and you have."

Jeanne had never told her grandmother or anyone about that horrible dream, but somehow her grandmother knew all about it.

But how?

Did Jeanne's grandfather have a mini heart attack the night before the big one that killed him? Did he communicate with his favorite granddaughter and his wife somehow? How did Jeanne and her grandmother have the same dream, and how did Jeanne have a dream about her grandfather's heart being stabbed only hours before he died of a heart attack?

***

The American mystic Edgar Cayce once said, "Dreams are *today's* answers to *tomorrow's* questions." Keep that in mind as I tell you the next story, which also kicks off with a dream.

In "Technicolor Dreams," from *Chicken Soup for the Soul: Dreams and Premonitions*, Susan Friel-Williams tells us about a perplexing dream. She is walking into her neighborhood Albertson's store when her friend and co-worker, Vicki, comes out, sobbing. Susan grabs her and says, "Vicki, what's wrong?" And Vicki answers, "Oh my God, Susan, I can't believe he's gone. I just can't believe he's gone!"

Susan woke up from this dream having no idea what to do. She couldn't very well warn Vicki that something bad was on the horizon. She didn't even know who Vicki had been referring to in the dream. Plus it was just a dream. But it bothered Susan and she told some of her friends at work and they decided to prepare *just in case*. They made a pact to be there for Vicki if she ever needed them, exchanging home phone numbers.

Several months passed and nothing happened. Susan's dream had not come true. Then, one night, Susan's husband came home and told her that he had a new employee he was training. She was deaf, so he needed help explaining things to her. He asked Susan if she knew anyone who had a basic sign language manual he could borrow. The first person that popped into Susan's head was Vicki, whose daughter was deaf.

> *"Dreams are today's answers to tomorrow's questions."*

Susan called Vicki at home for the first time and Vicki picked up, crying. Susan said, "Vicki, what's wrong?" and Vicki replied, "Oh my God, Susan, I can't believe he's gone. I just can't believe he's gone!"

The hair stood up on the back of Susan's neck. These were the exact words in her dream several months before. Vicki went on to explain that she had given birth to a son when she was younger and she had put him up for adoption. She had just learned that he had been killed in a car accident the night before. She couldn't afford the plane ticket to fly across the country to his funeral.

This was why Susan had created that *just in case* support group of co-workers. She reached out to them and within four hours they had purchased an airline ticket for Vicki.

When Vicki returned from her trip to the funeral, she called Susan to thank her. She also asked why Susan had been calling her that morning. They were friends at work, but had never expanded that to socializing, so Vicki wondered why Susan had been calling her at home. Susan explained about the new employee and how her husband wanted a basic sign language book so he could train her.

And wouldn't you know it? That new employee who worked

for Susan's husband and prompted that phone call was Vicki's own deaf daughter.

So, we have a premonition in a dream and a coincidence at work that prompted a phone call that made the dream into a reality.

But of course, some would say there are no coincidences in this world. They might say that Susan's dream and the impetus for her phone call to Vicki on the day she learned of her son's death were carefully orchestrated by forces we don't understand.

***

I feel like a kid at Show and Tell. Now that I have you here, I want to show you one more story!

"Jesse in the Sky" was published in *Chicken Soup for the Soul: Hope & Miracles* and it's one of the most heartbreaking and unexplainable stories I've heard.

It's the story of Scarlett Lewis, who lost her six-year-old son in that horrific Sandy Hook elementary school shooting in Newtown, Connecticut on December 14, 2012. I still remember the exact moment I heard about that because Newtown is actually in our county. Two of the people I've mentioned in this book were affected by it, actually. Our snowplow guy, who I mentioned in Chapter 16, lost his little nephew that day, and Sophfronia Scott, my smiling friend who I mentioned in Chapter 2, lost her godson, who was also a good friend of her son's. While the shooting was occurring in the first grade, Sophfronia's son Tain was in the building too, in his third grade classroom.

Jesse Lewis was one of the heroes that day. While he stood facing the killer, he yelled to his classmates to run. Those kids got away but Jesse's own path was blocked by that poor excuse for a human being, that gunman, who went ahead and shot him in the head.

Scarlett says that she and Jesse's older brother J.T. and other family members received dozens of little signs from him after he died — flickering lights, notes that he wrote that appeared out of the blue with the J in Jesse written backwards the way that Jesse always wrote it… these were little signs that might be viewed as coincidences but that Scarlett felt were little *Hellos* from Jesse.

About two weeks after the shooting, Scarlett decided to take J.T. to Orlando to get away, experience some warmth, and maybe help the healing process. She had more signs from Jesse on the flight. Jesse's favorite songs kept popping up on the in-flight music selection and then one of Scarlett's own favorites — Rick Springfield's "Jessie's Girl" — started playing.

When Scarlett arrived at the Orlando airport, she checked her phone and found a text message from a psychic who had befriended her. This message upset Scarlett because the psychic basically said that Scarlett might be holding Jesse back from heaven. She was always looking for signs from Jesse and that could be stopping him from moving on.

Scarlett told J.T. to wait for her at the car rental desk after she read that text. She ran into the ladies room to sob. It was typical mother's guilt. Her son was dead and she was still feeling responsible for his welfare. Now she was grief-stricken that she might have done something selfish to keep him with her. Was she preventing him from moving on to heaven?

Scarlett spoke out loud to Jesse in a stall in the ladies room and asked him to send a sign that he was okay. She asked him to let her know that he was with Jesus. And then she dried her tears and went off to get the rental car with her son J.T.

They had only been driving down the highway from the airport for a few minutes when they saw it.

A small plane was soaring across the blue sky. It was one of those skywriting planes. And it had spelled out something in smoke:

JESSE & JESUS. TOGETHER FOREVER.

And the "J" in "Jesse" was backwards — the same way Jesse used to write his name.

It gives you goose bumps, doesn't it?

Scarlett took a quick snapshot of the skywriting before it completely disappeared, and you can see the photo in the book that she wrote with Natasha Stoynoff — *Nurturing Healing Love*.

To Scarlett, this was a miraculous sign from heaven that her boy was okay. It made all the difference in her survival and healing after Jesse's death.

***

Whether you think these events were coincidences or whether you believe they involve divine intervention, angels whispering in someone's ear, ESP, or intuition, they make for great stories. And I find they enrich our lives by opening our hearts to *possibilities* — that something, somehow, somewhere can work in our lives to make good things happen when we need them most.

A Life of Yes, Yes, Yes

Stepping outside your comfort zone
will open up the world to you

I went to one of those rock-climbing gyms with my daughter a couple of years ago. I had decided around the time I turned fifty that I was going to start saying "yes" to as many new things as possible, but now I was afraid. It was scary to climb the beginner's wall, forcing myself to reach for the next handhold and relying on the harness to support me if I fell. But it was also fun, and I was glad that I did it. My upper back killed me for days afterwards, but now I understand what happens at a climbing gym and I will do it again if presented with the opportunity.

This new policy of saying "yes" had started when Bill and I finally went to the new cinema in the town next to ours. When it first opened we heard about it from my brother and some friends: it had stadium seating, fourteen screens, and IMAX. It was the best place to see movies in our area. But for two years, we didn't go.

Why? Because we hadn't been to this new area; we didn't know where to park; the town of Port Chester, New York was undergoing a redevelopment boom and we didn't know what had changed.

It was ridiculous. Finally we went, and of course it was terrific and there is lots of easy, free parking, and wonderful nearby restaurants. Now that is where we go to the movies.

I think that we had fallen into a rut and we had become awfully risk-averse. We had been working from home for several years at that point. Bill was consulting and I was serving on the board of directors of several publicly traded technology companies, all struggling start-ups. One week, two of my companies couldn't make payroll on the same Friday! I had to lend money to both of them. We had enough risk in our lives!

But going to the new movie theater was the beginning of us emerging from our cocoon. Soon thereafter, when I was dawdling on making reservations for our annual wedding anniversary trip, a guy at a cocktail party mentioned that it was a great time to go to Dubai. Everything was going bust, construction had ground to a halt, and the hotels were offering rooms at half their normal prices. With only two weeks to go, I dropped the idea of a Caribbean or Hawaiian vacation, and off we went on a wonderful adventure, complete with indoor skiing at the mall, dining alone in the desert with scorpions surrounding our torch-lit Persian carpet, and slaloming down the sand dunes in a Toyota Land Cruiser driven by a crazy twenty-year-old South African guide.

***

My new resolve to shake things up was strengthened when I read a story called "GO 60" that Susan Tornga wrote for *Chicken Soup for the Soul: Inspiration for the Young at Heart*. Susan decided that she would try sixty new things the year after she turned sixty and she would keep a diary listing all her experiences. Because she traveled frequently, many of the entries in her diary involved trying new things in exotic locations. She climbed the Sydney Harbour Bridge, licked a green ant in the rainforest, and drove a car on the left side of the road in Australia. She ate a new food — *pierogies* — in Gdansk, Poland. She toured the Hermitage museum in St. Petersburg, Russia. She climbed a steep trail to the top of Diamond Head on the island of Oahu in Hawaii.

> *Susan decided that she would try sixty new things the year after she turned sixty.*

Closer to home, she waterskied on Lake Powell, took a Mexican cooking class, figured out the gas grill when her husband wasn't home, and cranked out homemade pasta for the first time. She worked at the polls on Election Day, started a blog, and watched horse racing.

As Susan neared her sixty-first birthday, she had only fifty-four items on her list of new things. So she signed up for docent training at a local museum and sponge-painted a bathroom.

Susan says that in her zeal to put sixty items on her list, she agreed to do many things she would normally have turned down, including the Sydney Harbour Bridge climb, in which you take the steel stairs of the bridge up to its peak 440 feet over the water. (I've done it, too, but I am blessed with no fear of heights.)

According to Susan, "The unquestionable success of my GO 60 year was the shift in my mindset. I might never have agreed to the bridge climb, which, by the way, was not the least bit frightening once we got underway, had I not been looking to add to The

List. What a pity it would have been to miss the exhilaration and beauty of that experience."

Susan's story inspired me to make similar choices. I've tooled around Bermuda on a moped, zip-lined in Costa Rica, and dune-surfed again in Dubai on a second trip there even though I was terrified the first time. I might not have done these things if I hadn't been conscious of the need to keep stepping out of my comfort zone. I've tried new kinds of clothing, new drinks, and new foods. When we were launching our line of treats in our pet food business, I ate a dog biscuit in the office. We were trying them. Why not? It tasted like a rather healthy cookie.

It's so easy to get in a rut, doing the same things every year, rejecting anything new. Over time, we run the risk that our lives will get narrower and narrower, and that we'll start to fall behind — we won't understand references to what's in the news, our bodies will become less useful, and we won't avail ourselves of convenient new technologies. We might become boring — to ourselves and to other people. We might even lose touch with who we used to be — those vibrant, curious people we remember.

***

You may be wondering about my enthusiasm for saying "yes" when I wrote a whole chapter about the power of saying "no." The difference is that you're saying "yes" for *yourself* — to do things that make you a happier, more confident, more dynamic person. In fact, by using the power of no to reclaim command of your calendar, you make time to start saying "yes" to these new adventures.

The Nobel Prize–winning, French author André Gide said, "It is only in adventure that some people succeed in knowing themselves — in finding themselves." There is indeed a transformational power in saying "yes." In fact, if you make an overall policy decision — *I will say yes to everything that sounds interesting except things that are dangerous or stupid*—it's almost easier. You won't have to think about it. You'll just say yes. That's what Ericka Kahler did, as she explains in "The Summer of Yes," which we published in *Chicken Soup for the Soul: Time to Thrive.*

Ericka was in a writers' group that was losing members because they weren't booking interesting speakers for their meetings. Ericka offered to help and then got annoyed when no one else volunteered.

She did it herself and she cold-called someone interesting. That person, surprisingly, said he would speak at their meeting. Ericka thought, *Wow. That was so easy. Why couldn't anyone else do that?* Then she realized, it wasn't that no one else *could* do it; it was that no one else *did*.

Ericka had another realization. How many opportunities had she lost out on because she hadn't even tried?

Then she did something very cool. She decided that for the whole summer that stretched before her she would say "yes" to anything that was offered to her. Yes, she would walk a 5K race for charity. Yes, she would attend an outdoor concert. Yes, she would go to a science-fiction convention. Everything that sounded fun got a Yes.

Ericka discovered that she was doing and enjoying things that she had never dreamed of doing. "Yes" became her mantra. She would respond to every invitation with, "Of course, it's the Summer of Yes!" She even started looking for new things to try. She entered a costume contest. She rode her bicycle to work instead of driving. She experimented with new recipes.

She was such an inspiration to her friends that they started trying new things themselves. And then Ericka started saying yes to even bigger things, not only one-time events: She took on the presidency of her writers' group. She took courses in Database Administration. She submitted stories to publishers. She applied for a new job.

Ericka's Summer of Yes focused her on the things she really

wanted. She says she felt her real life had finally begun.

By the end of the year, Ericka had a new job, she was a published author, and she had earned her Associate's degree. She says that simple resolution — to say yes — changed her life.

The Summer of Yes turned into the Year of Yes and then Ericka's new Life of Yes. Ericka concludes her tale with an update: "I'm still saying 'yes' even though the tasks have gotten harder. 'Yes' got me a stellar performance review and a promotion. 'Yes' is taking me to Europe for the first time."

* * *

Ericka learned to say yes and expand her world. But what do you do when someone *gives* you a gift or an experience that is outside your comfort zone, something you didn't get to choose? Years ago, someone gave me a beaded bra that you were supposed to wear under a sheer blouse so that everyone could see it. *No thank you. Not my style.* But when one of my editors gave me purple nail polish, my first departure from classic beige, pink, or red, at first I was hesitant. Was I too old? Obviously, *she* didn't think I was. So I got excited and decided to join the modern world. I wore that purple nail polish for a couple of months, including during a TV interview about our book that we made with the Alzheimer's Association, which uses purple as its signature color.

Sometimes, what you view as an unwanted gift is actually a positive development in your new world of Yes, Yes, Yes — that good habit that keeps you engaged and growing. Nancy Hatten taught me that in her story called "The Gift of Change," which we published in *Chicken Soup for the Soul: Find Your Happiness.*

For years, Nancy was unhappy with most of the gifts she received for her birthday, Christmas, or other occasions. She says, "I put a lot of thought into the gifts I gave to others, and it seemed to me that they did not return the favor."

Why didn't Nancy's friends and family know that she didn't read romance novels? Or that she didn't like weird little gadgets for her car? And how come they didn't know that the only edible gift she wanted was chocolate?

"I didn't speak up," she says. "I didn't want to hurt the feelings of those I loved and cared about, but my resentment began to grow. I felt like the most important people in my life didn't really know me, or maybe didn't care enough about me to think about my likes and dislikes."

Then, one day, Nancy unwrapped a birthday gift from her teenage son, Jason. It was a blouse way more stylish than what she normally wore. She looked over at Jason and saw that he was smiling. He was excited about the gift he had chosen for her.

"What do you think, Mom?" asked Jason. "I thought it would look so nice on you."

Surprisingly, Nancy meant it when she answered, "It's beautiful." Because she finally understood: Jason was giving her a beautiful blouse for the person he thought she could *enjoy being*, not the stick-in-the-mud person she had become.

Jason believed better of his mom than she believed of herself. He saw her as a woman who would be willing to try something new, something *nicer*, *fancier*, and *more elegant* than what she normally allowed herself to wear. This was a *thoughtful gift* — a *fabulous* gift. Nancy finally understood the point of all those gifts that were outside her comfort zone.

When Nancy tried on that new blouse for Jason, he had no idea why she had tears in her eyes. It was because she knew, with sudden clarity, that he had given her so much more than a pretty blouse.

After this change in perspective, Nancy thought about all the gifts she'd privately rejected over the years, and she realized that the gift givers saw something in her that she hadn't seen in herself. Maybe they thought she was more adventurous than she was, more romantic, more creative in the kitchen… and why not? Nancy decided that the gifts that seemed a little off, which were not quite her, were truly the best gifts of all—gifts that would open her mind to change and growth.

Now Nancy loves *all* the gifts she receives, no matter how out of left field they seem to be. She no longer sees them as evidence that her friends and family don't know the real her, or that they aren't trying to please her. They're seeing the Nancy that she can *become*, the one who is happy to try new things. She enthusiastically says "yes" to the new Nancy these gifts represent.

*** *** ***

I haven't talked about "accountability" at all in this book, but I'm going to mention it right now so that you will be my accountability partner for the next scary thing that I'm going to try—my next big Yes. You know what an accountability partner is, right? It's someone you tell about your resolution and then you are accountable to that person and you *have to do* whatever you said you would do.

> *"Twenty years from now you will be more disappointed by the things that you didn't do than by the ones you did do."*

Here's my scary thing: In November, Bill and I have a business trip to Dubai and we're going to take advantage of the trip to go on a short vacation to a very cool, beachside resort in nearby Oman.

The resort in Oman is so remote that when you drive there, you have three choices for the last part of the trip: 1) arriving by speedboat; 2) transferring from the car to a four-wheel drive vehicle to go the last five kilometers down a winding mountain road to the beach; or, 3) jumping off a 1,000-foot-high mountain cliff and paragliding down to Reception, where they hand you a well deserved cocktail when you land. According to tripadvisor.

com, the really cool guests arrive by paraglider.

So, inspired by Ericka's "Yes" strategy and Susan's "Go 60" year, I impetuously booked the paragliders for us. Bill was excited and I felt pretty adventurous.

Now I've had *months* to think about jumping off that cliff and there are still months of nervous anticipation — and time to back out — ahead of me. But now you know about it too, so it's definitely happening. That's how having an accountability partner works.

Mark Twain once said: "Twenty years from now you will be more disappointed by the things that you didn't do than by the ones you did do. So throw off the bowlines. Sail away from the safe harbor. Catch the trade winds in your sails. Explore. Dream. Discover."

Once you make the decision to step outside your comfort zone — to take the leap — it can start close to home, with venturing into new neighborhoods for a movie or rock climbing indoors in a gym. Pretty soon the Yeses will have it, and you're jumping off cliffs in the Middle East.

A life of yes, yes, and more yes is about keeping your confident, compassionate, cheerful self on the path of happiness and adventure and wellbeing.

Why I Do What I Do... and How

A privilege, a responsibility, and a "ministry"

This is an insanely busy job for me to have undertaken just as our last child was going off to college. After all, my hectic life had been on the verge of slowing down. But I've poured my heart and soul into this for nine years and I'm grateful for every minute of it.

Why do I do it? Because, as all-consuming as it is, this is a fabulous opportunity to do what I've always loved — read and write — *and* make a difference in the lives of millions of people.

There's an old saying: "Choose a job you love, and you will never have to work a day in your life." That's how I feel... most days. Then, of course, there are those tough days when I can't believe that I *chose* to work *this hard*!

Robert Frost explained it very well: "By working faithfully eight hours a day you may eventually get to be boss and work twelve hours a day." Bill and I do work very long hours virtually every day. And so do many of our people. I have to laugh when D'ette Corona or Barbara LoMonaco send me e-mails confessing they are going to take a vacation day, except that they're writing about a *Saturday* or a *Sunday. Hello...* Taking off a Saturday or a Sunday does not count as a vacation day!

Bill and I have to be particularly careful that we don't let work take over our lives and our marriage. I'm in charge of creating our books, and he oversees *everything*, including our other businesses, which include the pet food and television businesses. We also have a lot of overlapping responsibilities and we are constantly consulting with each other about decisions, and sometimes disagreeing.

Technically, Bill is my boss. (I hear you laughing.) No, really.

It's Saturday morning as I'm writing this, and Bill just got up. I've been working on this manuscript for three hours already. *Just saying.*

Anyway, I'd been waiting a few weeks for my "annual review" and Bill kept putting it off. I just now asked him what ever happened to my review. He responded, "You're beautiful. That's it." *Okay, then.* Thanks, Boss.

> "Choose a job you love, and you will never have to work a day in your life."

People always ask how we can work together all day, spend our nights and weekends together, and not kill each other. Believe it or not, we always say we want to go on vacation so we can spend *more* time together. I'm not sure I understand it myself.

Actually, we are so passionate about what we do that we have a built-in sympathy for each other's obsession with work and we don't mind talking about it. But we also try to respect each other's right to say *enough is enough* when we need a break.

Here's how we do it. If you saw any of the Harry Potter movies or read the books, you'll remember that the evil wizard Voldemort was so terrifying that everyone but the equally powerful wizard Harry Potter called him "He-Who-Must-Not-Be-Named."

So through some bizarre husband/wife shared brainwave activity, we both decided that, occasionally, work — Chicken Soup for the Soul — would be "He-Who-Must-Not-Be-*Discussed*," a bit like Voldemort. When either of us is sick of talking about work at night or on weekends, we can "Declare Voldemort" and the other person is not allowed to discuss work *at all*.

This often happens on a Friday night. "Voldemort" remains in effect until Monday morning. Bill is not even allowed to text me a question about work when Voldemort is in effect, because texting is too much like talking. We might be sitting next to each other at the kitchen table, working on our computers, but we have to *e-mail* each other our questions. I've made it perfectly clear to him that if I don't want to answer one of those e-mails until Monday, when we are "back at work," then I don't have to!

"Declaring Voldemort" works for us, and there is still plenty to talk about. Just because we enjoy working together doesn't mean we don't have a normal marriage. Bill still asks me where things are in the kitchen, items that have been in the same place for two decades. He asks what he should eat while he's looking in the refrigerator. He asks me what to wear, what time we are leaving, and where we are going.

Like any good wife, I refuse to answer his questions until he "needs to know" because he won't listen to my answers anyway. All in all, it's a perfectly normal marriage, despite the evil Voldemort's regular appearances.

In addition to Voldemort, we have other little traditions that we use to take back ownership of at least a bit of our lives. On Sundays, we are adamant that we have a big fancy breakfast together, usually involving something with maple syrup, and we call those Sinful Sundays.

And we absolutely have to be on vacation for our wedding anniversary every November. It doesn't matter what is happening in the business — this vacation is sacred. I instituted this mandatory tradition after a disappointing wedding anniversary early in our marriage. Bill forced me to go to an incredibly boring black tie dinner, with no dancing and only speeches. He was somewhere else in the ballroom performing his duties as one of the board members of this particular nonprofit while I sat alone at our table with six accountants from Verizon.

* * *

My favorite part of the job is making the books. All the business stuff — the royalty spreadsheets, the coauthor contracts, the sales and marketing, the manufacturing of the books — is what I have to endure in order to do what I love most: picking the stories and editing them into a rich, useful, entertaining book. It is such a privilege to work with these stories and these writers.

Without our writers, we wouldn't have anything.

> I am still blown away after all these years by how positive, resourceful, and resilient our writers are.

These people unselfishly share their stories even when they're exposing a personal flaw or something embarrassing. Sometimes they reveal deeply personal moments in their lives that they have never even shared with their families or friends. That's exactly what happened to me while writing this book! I couldn't believe how many personal stories I shared with you in these pages. I hadn't expected to do it, but the rest of our writers do it, so it's my turn.

Whenever I can find time on my schedule, I meet with our writers — our "contributors" — in the U.S. and Canada. It's such a privilege to meet the people behind the stories and thank them personally. Bill has come to some of these events and he says my face absolutely glows when I am talking to our writers. These are my people! I already feel like I know them from reading the stories they submit, so it's a thrill to put names and faces together.

We've hosted a couple dozen of these contributor luncheons and dinners in the last few years and I'm eager to do more. Here are photos from two of them, the first in Los Angeles and the second in Toronto.

Picking stories that might influence people's lives is a big responsibility. We get e-mails and letters all the time from people telling us that our books have helped them do the right thing, been a friend when they thought they were alone, caused them to pick up the phone and call an estranged relative or friend... or even that we have stopped them from considering suicide. When we get one of *those* e-mails it further drives home the huge responsibility that we have.

We normally receive about 5,000 submissions for the 101 slots in each book. Why 101? That is a legacy from Jack Canfield and Mark Victor Hansen. They wanted to give people 100 stories, and then *one more*... to keep propelling them forward.

How do those stories come in? We post what we're looking for on our website — chickensoup.com — and that's where people go to fill out a form and submit their stories as well.

It's uncomfortable to reject stories, especially since we know and like so many of the writers, but we have to reject about 4,900 stories to make every book. That's why it's such a big deal to get in and that's why our writers are often featured in their local newspapers or on local TV when we publish their stories. Some writers spend years submitting to us; others make it in, miraculously, on their first try. A number of our writers have published ten or more stories with us — a few as many as twenty or thirty over our twenty-three-year history.

How do we choose the 101 stories that ultimately grace the pages of each book? There *is* an overarching imperative, and that is to introduce you to positive people whose stories illustrate *simple* ways to have a *happier* life. Positive people give us stories that are empowering and uplifting, encouraging our readers to look within themselves for the keys to being happy, productive, and purposeful. I love stories from people who have been through enormous challenges and yet have maintained a constructive attitude, filled with gratitude for the good things they still have.

You won't find any narcissists among our writers. They're not big complainers either. I think that my attitude toward people in general has changed after working on these books. People are amazing! I am still blown away after all these years by how positive, resourceful, and resilient our writers are. They are wonderful role models for all of us at Chicken Soup for the Soul and they've changed my life.

***

Many people have told me that what we do is a "ministry." And in a non-religious way, they are correct. I looked up the definition in *Merriam-Webster* and the multiple definitions include:

1) "the office, duties, or functions of a minister," and
2) "a person or thing through which something is accomplished"

In a way, we minister to our readers through our books. And, also, we try to accomplish things through our philanthropic work. These days it seems like every company says it's socially conscious, but I promise we really are! We support a large number of nonprofits through royalty payments from our books, including the Alzheimer's Association and American Humane Association, but we also raise funds for autism research, children's afterschool programs, cancer research, programs for veterans, and many other wonderful causes. The two areas that occupy the most time for me are our bullying prevention program, which is sponsored by the Boniuk Foundation, and our work with shelters to support the adoption of dogs and cats.

A couple of our very religious coauthors were talking to me about this "ministry" concept last year and they asked if I went to church or temple or any place of worship regularly. I mumbled something about *Sinful Sunday* (you know, our special breakfast), and *work*, and *grown children who need to be visited* in all the *unauthorized* places they are living that are far from Greenwich, Connecticut where we live. And then I braced myself to hear some kindhearted suggestions about how I should undertake *some kind* of formal religious tradition.

But they never came. Instead, both women said something to the effect of: "You should just keep doing what you're doing. I love it and I understand your mission. It's more important for you to spend those hours doing *your* work than it is for you to go to church on Sunday morning."

And, I thought, *that's what keeps me doing what I do.*

You Already Have
Your Toolkit

Everything you need to improve your
life is already inside you

think you've gotten the point now. In our world — the
Chicken Soup for the Soul world of self-help or self-
improvement or whatever you want to call it — you don't
have to attend seminars, fill out workbooks, or pay expensive coaches to help you become a happier, more productive person. You don't have to devote months to implementing the ideas
in this book, either. Most of them can be adopted in minutes,
or even seconds, just by deciding to view something differently.
These are simple ideas that you can use immediately to have a
happy life.

You already have your toolkit. Everything you need to improve
your life is already *inside* you. You can be your own life's "mechanic."

What I've learned from my life and from reading more than
20,000 Chicken Soup for the Soul stories is that we are all way
better equipped than we believe. All of our writers, who started
out as ordinary people and then had some kind of extraordinary
experience, would tell you that they didn't know they had it in them.

Here's what you already have in your toolkit:

- Wise self-knowledge that you haven't fully tapped
- More resilience and courage than you ever imagined

- The self-discipline that you thought you lacked
- More likeability than you gave yourself credit for
- Long buried passion that can give you purpose
- A sense of adventure that will keep you dynamic
- Intellectual curiosity that never has to stop wowing you
- A willingness to change and grow
- Energy to bound forward and greet each day with vigor
- As many smiles as you need to send out there
- The ability to make decisions to change… instantly
- A deep well of forgiveness and compassion
- A sense of humor that will help you through tough times
- Creativity that you can use to redefine the negative
- People who will be happy to help you if you ask

As Jack Canfield says, "There are essentially two things that will make you wise — the books you read and the people you meet." I hope this book has made you *doubly* wise because of the stories you read *and* the people you met in its pages.

Putting this book together was a great way for me to review all these Chicken Soup for the Soul lessons and renew my faith in my own toolkit.

Let's recap our journey through twenty-three years of Chicken Soup for the Soul advice and wisdom by recalling where we've been:

In Chapter 1, we learned that every little thing we do matters and makes a difference. It's always worth it.

In Chapter 2, we saw how easy it is to add smiling to your life. It can change your whole day and have a marvelous ripple effect.

In Chapter 3, we learned to stifle our negative inner voices and our biggest critics — ourselves.

In Chapter 4, we learned that we should strive for excellence, but not perfection, because perfection is a losing game.

In Chapter 5, we learned to re-integrate our minds with our bodies — to love and nurture and use those bodies.

In Chapter 6, we learned that you can *pretend* to be who you want to be, the type of person you want to be — and *become* that person.

In Chapter 7, we learned there's nothing wrong with expecting great things of people because they will rise to the challenge.

In Chapter 8, we learned to be bold, speak up, and follow our gut even when it's embarrassing or inconvenient.

In Chapter 9, we learned how much you can accomplish in sixty seconds, and how to use those found minutes.

In Chapter 10, we learned how to find happiness and bring purpose and passion into our lives.

In Chapter 11, we learned that our dreams are a window into what we already know but are too distracted to hear.

In Chapter 12, we learned to dare to be different when raising children, as there's nothing wrong with being weird. It works.

In Chapter 13, we learned why we should always listen to our mothers, even if they are no longer with us.

In Chapter 14, I revealed why I would be the world's worst therapist and how to put things in perspective.

In Chapter 15, we learned how to use the power of gratitude to make us happier, healthier, and more successful.

In Chapter 16, we saw that we can redefine anything and make it better so as to navigate life's ups and downs.

In Chapter 17, we learned the merit of performing good deeds and why the biggest beneficiaries will be ourselves.

In Chapter 18, we learned how to do some of those good deeds for ourselves and to treat ourselves as well as a guest.

In Chapter 19, we learned how to use the power of saying "no" to de-clutter our calendars and our homes.

In Chapter 20, we took that one step further by saying "no" to the toxic people and "frenemies" in our lives.

In Chapter 21, we learned not to take things personally and to remember that it's almost never about us.

In Chapter 22, we picked up some easy tips for reducing stress, even for those of us who are extreme multitaskers.

In Chapter 23, we learned the importance of the power of forgiveness and the imperative to use it to free ourselves.

In Chapter 24, we confronted the unexplainable, and learned that mysterious and wonderful things can happen and we just need to accept them.

And, finally, in Chapter 25, after clearing the road to our futures, we talked about a life filled with saying "yes" to new challenges, experiences, and fun — and stepping outside our comfort zones!

Because, as Thomas Edison said, "If we all did the things we are capable of doing, we would literally astound ourselves."

Thank you for joining me on this journey,

Amy Newmark

ACKNOWLEDGMENTS

'd venture to say that Chicken Soup for the Soul was one of the first companies to engage in "crowdsourcing," which is all the buzz today. We would be nothing without the stories that are sent in by the hundreds every day. They form the basis for everything we do. Therefore, my first thanks go out to our wonderful writers — our "contributors." There are about 10,000 of them out there. Their selfless sharing, their keen insights, their wit, and their spirit are inspiring for all of us who work on these books.

Next up is my editorial team, led by Associate Publisher D'ette Corona and Senior Editor Barbara LoMonaco, who are the original "Chickens" who taught me everything when I came in as a newbie publisher in 2008. They have become my close friends as well as valued colleagues. Kristiana Glavin Pastir joined the editorial team shortly after I did in 2008, and she was by my side through thick and thin until she went off to have twins last year. We value every hour she can spare for us now, especially since she's adding a third grammar-geek-in-training to her family shortly.

I am blessed with an incredible team that contributed directly to this book's creation: Victor Cataldo, who heads up production and special projects; Dan Zaccari, our very patient and creative graphic designer who has re-energized our look; Mary Fisher, my executive assistant who acts as an editor too; Maureen Peltier, who handles the marketing side of our business; and Ronelle Frankel, who edits and organizes and can do anything that we ask of her. Everyone at Chicken Soup for the Soul contributes to the publishing effort but special thanks go to our Senior VP Joelle Jarvis, who persuaded me to write this book in the first place.

I also need to thank Dawn Aquino, my husband's assistant,

who buys us groceries and does anything she can think of to help us out. There's also Jon Brodsky, who helps me with my podcast and anything Internet, Maria Pappa, who helps me with social media, Amanda Romaniello, who was in on the early days of this book's genesis, and countless others at the company. They are all friends and amazing colleagues.

I also want to thank Jeff Schwartz and Alan Eisenson at MMG Management Group for encouraging me to do the podcast, and Chad Dougatz for producing it. As I said in the book, it was the podcast that opened the floodgates and allowed me to find the voice that enabled me to finally write this book.

Also in the outside world, we are blessed to have a wonderful group of "coauthors" who help us with story selection, editing, and PR. They have helped us maintain our rigorous publication schedule, they have unearthed great stories for us, and they have all become friends. In recent years, they have included Deborah Norville, Brooke Burke-Charvet, Susan Heim, LeAnn Thieman, Kelly Sullivan Walden, Jennifer Quasha, Joan Lunden, Dean Karnazes, Janet Matthews, Kevin Sorbo, Anthony Anderson, Jo Dee Messina, Loren Slocum Lahav, Claire Cook, Dr. Carolyn Roy-Bernstein, and Natasha Stoynoff.

And that brings me to Natasha Stoynoff, who deserves a special callout for guiding me through the whole writing process, because it was very different from editing one of our normal *Chicken Soup for the Soul* books. Natasha spent two solid weeks in my house helping me create the Table of Contents, "interviewing" me to get those personal stories to come out, and editing this editor. She was my coach, my cheerleader, my teacher, my confidante, and my good friend every step of the way.

Finally, there's my family. My husband Bill Rouhana suffered through all my angst, late nights, the takeover of the dining room, and all the stories I told about him throughout these pages. He always believes I can do the impossible, and then he makes me do it. And there are our wonderful children, who in addition to providing fodder for my writing, never cease to amaze me with their own adventures. Thank you, Ella, Mike, Rosey, and Tim, and your equally amazing partners Josh, Emily, and Joey. I love you and thank you for your stories and your support. And Mike, thanks for telling me I wasn't done when I thought I was, for being my final editor, and for making me change the title of the book on the way to the printer!

I'm pleased to introduce you to the writers of the stories that I referred to in the book. Here they are, along with their bios at the time their stories were published by us.

Shannon Anderson has her Master of Education degree and lives in Indiana where she enjoys spending time with her family, running, writing, teaching, presenting, and learning. She taught first grade for sixteen years and is currently an elementary literacy coach and high ability coordinator. E-mail her at shannonisteaching@gmail.com. *Chicken Soup for the Soul: Find Your Happiness (2011)*

Beth Arvin began writing plays for her siblings and neighborhood friends in grammar school. Currently she writes a daily blog, betharvin365.livejournal.com, and a blog, "I Think So," for the *Kent Reporter*. She is hoping to complete her first novel by mid 2012. E-mail her at betharvin@gmail.com. *Chicken Soup for the Soul: Say Goodbye to Stress (2012)*

Jeanne Blandford has found her dream job as an editor at Chicken Soup for the Soul. When she is not reading inspirational submissions, she and her husband, Jack, are visiting their two children; working on documentaries; writing and producing children's books or volunteering for OPIN, a local animal rescue. *Chicken Soup for the Soul: Messages from Heaven (2012)*

Janet Newlan Bower is a retired professor of history teaching for over thirty years. Her publications include contributing a chapter to *Women in the Biological Sciences: A Bibliographic Sourcebook*, *Tigerpaper*, *National Parks and Conservation*, *The Explorer*, *Environment Southwest* and *Child Life*, among others. Read her historical blog

at historyallaround.com.
Chicken Soup for the Soul: Time to Thrive (2015)

Elaine L. Bridge worked in the woods on the West Coast as a forester before becoming a stay-at-home mom to her three boys. Now living in Ohio she works part-time in a grocery store and is devoted to developing her relationship with God, caring for her family and writing inspirational material.
Chicken Soup for the Soul: Think Positive (2010)

Mary Wood Bridgman's work has appeared previously in *Chicken Soup for the Soul: Devotional Stories for Wives* as well as in many other publications. Mary has written two middle-grade books, for which she is seeking a literary agent. She is currently writing an adult mystery novel. E-mail her at marybridgman@msn.com.
Chicken Soup for the Soul: Thanks to My Mom (2015)

Douglas M. Brown has been writing since he was twelve years old. He has been published in several religious magazines, in *Chicken Soup for the Latter-day Saint Soul* and *Chicken Soup for the New Mom's Soul*. He lives in West Jordan, UT. You may contact Doug via e-mail at d8snraysons@yahoo.com.
Chicken Soup for the Soul: Shaping the New You (2010)

Cindy Charlton is a professional speaker and published author. She lives in Colorado with her two sons and adorable pooch, Lilly. Cindy invites you to visit her website, www.cindycharltonspeaks. com. She also writes a monthly blog, "The Survivor's Handbook," thesurvivorshandbook@blogsport.com.
Chicken Soup for the Soul: From Lemons to Lemonade (2013)

A.B. Chesler is a writer, educator, mommy, and wife from sunny Southern California. She enjoys reading, writing, traveling, and

finding happiness in the simple things. Feel free to contact her at achesler24@gmail.com or follow her blog at thishouseoflove.net.
Chicken Soup for the Soul: Hope & Miracles (2015)

Nikki Deckon lives in the Northwest with her husband, two spunky sons and three spirited cats. Her writing desk is right in the middle of all the action—the kitchen. Some day she hopes to be more like Mother Teresa and a woman that her boys admire. E-mail her at reachnikkideckon@yahoo.com.
Chicken Soup for the Soul: Think Positive (2010)

Drema Sizemore Drudge is a Spalding University MFA graduate. She is an agented author who primarily writes fiction about art. Drema and her husband Barry live in Indiana. Read more about her at dremadrudge.com.
Chicken Soup for the Soul: Dreams and Premonitions (2015)

Steve Erwin is an award-winning journalist and wrote the New York Times bestseller, *Left to Tell: Discovering God Amidst the Rwandan Genocide* with Immaculée Ilibagiza. He was an NYC correspondent for the Canadian Broadcasting Corporation and writer for *People* magazine. He's written seven nonfiction books and is finishing his second novel.
Chicken Soup for the Soul: The Power of Forgiveness (2014)

Tracy Fitzgerald married her best friend in December of 2010 and their daughter was born the summer of 2011. Tracy is a stay-at-home mom and enjoys painting pottery, traveling and spending time with her family.
Chicken Soup for the Soul: Reader's Choice 20th Anniversary Edition (2013)

Susan Friel-Williams is a licensed private investigator in Florida

who specializes in family search and reunion. She has appeared on *Oprah*, *CBS This Morning*, the *Today* show and most recently as a cast member on *The Locator*. She and her husband Lane Williams just celebrated their twenty-fifth wedding anniversary.
Chicken Soup for the Soul: Dreams and Premonitions (2015)

Christina Galeone is a freelance writer from New England. She enjoys writing regularly for Beliefnet, *The Catholic Free Press*, *Community Advocate* and the *Telegram & Gazette*. She also writes screenplays. She is excited to be included in this *Chicken Soup for the Soul* book!
Chicken Soup for the Soul: The Power of Forgiveness (2014)

James A. Gemmell spent most of his working life in industrial settings. Possibly as a result of this, he now spends as much time as possible outdoors — hiking, fishing, snowshoeing and walking continental camino routes. To date, he has racked up more than four thousand kilometers hiking in Spain and France.
Chicken Soup for the Soul: Hope & Miracles (2015)

Esther McNeil Griffin, a graduate of SUNY Geneseo, volunteers at the Ross Park Zoo in Binghamton, NY. She has written *Alex, the Lonely Black-Footed Penguin*, and written and illustrated *Which Witch is Which, Today?* and *My Mom Hates Violence*. E-mail her at Eltiemblo@aol.com.
Chicken Soup for the Soul: From Lemons to Lemonade (2013)

Judythe Guarnera connects with people through her volunteer work as a mediator and through her writing. Her first novel, *Twenty-Nine Sneezes*, is in the final editing stage. She has been published in a variety of venues, including a previous *Chicken Soup for the Soul* book.
Chicken Soup for the Soul: The Power of Forgiveness (2014)

Carolyn Hall received her bachelor's degree from Kansas State University. She and her husband live on a river bluff overlooking the Kansas River. She loves writing about her family, cooking and baking. E-mail her at chall711@gmail.com.
Chicken Soup for the Soul: Messages from Heaven (2012)

Nancy Hatten grew up in Belvidere, IL, where she enjoyed the change of seasons and fell in love with the Chicago Cubs. Now she lives in beautiful Austin, TX, where she often battles the heat but no longer snow and ice.
Chicken Soup for the Soul: Find Your Happiness (2011)

Immaculée Ilibagiza is the author, with Steve Erwin, of several books including the New York Times bestseller *Left to Tell: Discovering God Amidst the Rwandan Holocaust*. A recipient of the Mahatma Gandhi International Award for Peace and Reconciliation, she travels the world speaking about forgiveness. Please visit her website at www.immaculee.com.
Chicken Soup for the Soul: The Power of Forgiveness (2014)

Jennie Ivey lives in Cookeville, TN. She is the author of numerous works of fiction and nonfiction, including stories in several books of the *Chicken Soup for the Soul* series. Visit her website at www.jennieivey.com.
Chicken Soup for the Soul: The Power of Positive (2012)

Linda Jackson enjoys life with her husband Jeff and their three children. As an author, she enjoys spinning stories with small-town settings. Her debut novel, set in fictitious Stillwater, MS during the summer of 1955, is forthcoming from Houghton Mifflin Harcourt. Learn more at www.jacksonbooks.com.
Chicken Soup for the Soul: Dreams and Premonitions (2015)

Jeanie Jacobson is on the leadership team of Wordsowers Christian Writers in Omaha, NE. She's been published in seven *Chicken Soup for the Soul* books, and is writing a Christian-slanted fantasy series. Jeanie loves visiting family and friends, reading, hiking, praise dancing, and gardening. Learn more at jeaniejacobson.com.
Chicken Soup for the Soul: The Joy of Less (2016)

Jackson Jarvis is fourteen years old, into surfing and classic rock (he thinks he should've been born in the 60's). An aspiring music producer, he's also written three yet-to-be published books including *The Book of Bad Ideas* and *The Weird Stuff I Do*. He lives in New York State with his mom, Joelle, and his dad Eric is his guardian angel.
Chicken Soup for the Soul: Miraculous Messages from Heaven (2013)

Ruth Jones lives in Cookeville, TN, with her husband Terry and a very fat cat named Annabel.
Chicken Soup for the Soul: Find Your Happiness (2011)

Ericka Kahler has lived in eight states, each progressively farther north. She graduated from the University of West Florida with a B.A. degree in History in 1999. Ericka is now a web developer in Michigan, sharing her home with a husband and way too many dogs.
Chicken Soup for the Soul: Time to Thrive (2015)

Ginger Katz is the author of *Sunny's Story* and CEO/Founder of The Courage to Speak Foundation, a nonprofit founded after her son died of a drug overdose. She presents nationwide to break the silence about drug use and she spearheaded the development of drug education programs for students and parents. Learn more at www.couragetospeak.org.
Chicken Soup for the Soul: Find Your Inner Strength (2014)

April Knight is proud to be a contributor to the *Chicken Soup for*

the Soul series. She is currently writing romance novels for people over fifty. April spends her days riding horses and her nights writing mystery novels. She also writes a newspaper column and novels under her tribal name Crying Wind Hummingbird.
Chicken Soup for the Soul: Say Goodbye to Stress (2012)

Mimi Greenwood Knight is a "Luzianna" mother of four and freelance writer specializing in humorous essays on motherhood. Her collection, *Mom, You're Not Going to WRITE About This, Are You?*, is currently in search of a publisher. (Hello out there!) Mimi has essays in two-dozen *Chicken Soup for the Soul* books.
Chicken Soup for the Soul: Parenthood (2013)

This is **T. Jensen Lacey's** thirteenth story in the *Chicken Soup for the Soul* series. In addition, Lacey has published fourteen books and/ or novels and, as a freelance journalist, has published more than 800 articles for newspapers and magazines. She enjoys reading, hiking, being outdoors and cooking. E-mail her at TJensenLacey@ yahoo.com.
Chicken Soup for the Soul: The Joy of Less (2016)

Scarlett Lewis is the mother of Jesse Lewis, who was killed in his first grade classroom during the tragedy at Sandy Hook Elementary School. She founded the Jesse Lewis Choose Love Foundation and wrote the book *Nurturing Healing Love* based on a prophetic message her son wrote on their kitchen chalkboard.
Chicken Soup for the Soul: Hope & Miracles (2015)

Sydney Logan is an elementary school librarian and the best-selling author of six novels. A native of East Tennessee, she enjoys playing piano and relaxing on her porch with her wonderful husband and their very spoiled cat. Learn more at www.sydneylogan.com.
Chicken Soup for the Soul: The Joy of Less (2016)

Sara Matson lives in Minnesota with her husband and twin twelve-year-old daughters. Her stories have appeared in four other *Chicken Soup for the Soul* books. E-mail her at saramatsonstories@hotmail.com.
Chicken Soup for the Soul: The Power of Positive (2012)

Phyllis McKinley has one house, two citizenships, three step-grandchildren, four children, five grandchildren, and soon-to-be six books published. She has lived in seven houses in eight years and nine cities in ten years. She collects books, quotes and friends wherever she goes. E-mail her at leafybough@hotmail.com.
Chicken Soup for the Soul: The Joy of Less (2016)

Donna Milligan Meadows is the mother of six adult children—including triplets. She worked for many years as an elementary school librarian and hopes to write a children's book someday. She loves reading, traveling, gardening and especially reading to her grandchildren. E-mail her at meadowsdonna@hotmail.com.
Chicken Soup for the Soul: Think Positive (2010)

Andrew Nalian is the author of *50 Deeds for Those in Need*. He believes that if you focus on doing one good deed a day, the world will be rich with something money can't buy—happiness. If you were influenced by Andrew's story, he would love to hear from you at TheDeedDoctor@gmail.com.
Chicken Soup for the Soul: Find Your Inner Strength (2014)

Giulietta Nardone lives in Massachusetts with her husband and two cats. Her stories have been published in books, newspapers and broadcast on the radio. In addition to writing, Giulietta paints, sings, acts, hikes, bikes, travels and saves historic buildings. E-mail her at giuliettan@gmail.com.

Chicken Soup for the Soul: Reboot Your Life (2014)

Leah Shearer Noonan is a two-time cancer survivor, writer and wife who has worked both in nonprofit and education. Leah graduated from St. Bonaventure University in 2000 and has worked with teens with disabilities for over a decade. She speaks nationally on behalf of young adult cancer survivors.
Chicken Soup for the Soul: The Joy of Less (2016)

LaVerne Otis loves to write and is presently taking her first writing class at a local community college. She has been published in *Country* and *Birds and Blooms* magazines. Other hobbies include photography, bird watching, gardening and spending lots of time with her family. She can be contacted at lotiswrites@msn.com.
Chicken Soup for the Soul: Count Your Blessings (2009)

Robin Pressnall is Executive Director of Small Paws Rescue Inc., which is featured on Animal Planet's *Dogs 101*. She has been a three-time guest on the Fox News Network's *Fox & Friends* in NYC. Robin lives in Tulsa, OK, with her husband Dale, and their three Bichon Frises.
Chicken Soup for the Soul: Find Your Happiness (2011)

Connie Kaseweter Pullen lives in rural Sandy, OR, near her five children and several grandchildren. She received her Bachelor of Arts, *cum laude*, from the University of Portland in 2006, with a double major in Psychology and Sociology. Connie enjoys writing, photography and exploring the outdoors.
Chicken Soup for the Soul: Dreams and Premonitions (2015)

Joe Rector has published three books, along with several other pieces for magazines and newspapers, and writes a weekly personal

column for *The Knoxville Focus*, a weekly newspaper. E-mail him at joerector@comcast.net.
Chicken Soup for the Soul: The Power of Forgiveness (2014)

Anna Redsand is a retired educator and counselor. Her YA biography, *Viktor Frankl: A Life Worth Living* (Clarion, 2006), has received four awards. Her work has appeared in *Third Coast* magazine, *Friends Journal, Fireweed, Rockhurst Review*, and other periodicals. She lives in Albuquerque and writes full time.
Chicken Soup for the Soul: Inspiration for Writers (2013)

Mariah Reyes received the ABC7 Cool Kids award in 2014, worked for the U.S. Forest Service in the summer of 2015, and is currently a Youth Social Media Correspondent for the World Peace Caravan. Mariah loves to hike, sing and volunteer.
Chicken Soup for the Soul: Dreams and Premonitions (2015)

Johanna Richardson, always a lover of the written word, dabbles with writing for her own pleasure and is a voracious reader. Her life has been blessed by a wonderful husband and family. She is an RN, has a master's degree from the University of San Francisco, and is a Peer Volunteer for the National Alzheimer's Association.
Chicken Soup for the Soul: Touched by an Angel (2014)

Linda J. Rivers is a California native, now residing in the state of Minnesota with her husband Ernie, a retired military officer with the United States Army, and eleven-year-old daughter, Kira. She began her writing career in 1980 as a weekly columnist for the *Statesman Journal* newspaper in Salem, OR.
Chicken Soup for the Soul: Shaping the New You (2010)

Kathi Lessner Schafer is a Chicago native and lives in North Carolina with her daughter, husband, and two ungrateful cats. In addition

to homeschooling their daughter, she is actively involved with local wildlife conservation groups and natural habitat preservation.
Chicken Soup for the Soul: Think Positive (2010)

When **Sophfronia Scott** published her novel, *All I Need to Get By*, with St. Martin's Press, one reviewer referred to her as "one of the best writers of her generation." Her work has appeared in *Time*, *People, More*, NewYorkTimes.com, *Sleet Magazine, Numéro Cinq, Saranac Review* and *O, The Oprah Magazine*.
Chicken Soup for the Soul: Reader's Choice (2013)

Georgia Shaffer is a certified life coach, a licensed psychologist in Pennsylvania, and the author of *Taking Out Your Emotional Trash* and *A Gift of Mourning Glories*. As a professional speaker, she loves to encourage cancer survivors and healthcare givers. For more information, visit www.GeorgiaShaffer.com or e-mail her at Georgia@GeorgiaShaffer.com.
Chicken Soup for the Soul: Hope & Healing for Your Breast Cancer Journey (2012)

Dayle Allen Shockley is an award-winning writer whose by-line has appeared in dozens of publications. She is the author of three books and a contributor to many other works, including the *Chicken Soup for the Soul* series. E-mail her at dayle@dayleshockley.com.
Chicken Soup for the Soul: Count Your Blessings (2009)

Paula Klendworth Skory received her B.S. and M.S. degree, *summa cum laude*, from the University of North Texas. She is a registered CPA and lives in Washington, IL, where she and her husband raised their three children. She is the youngest of ten children, and a breast cancer survivor. She tries to find the beauty in the little moments of life.
Chicken Soup for the Soul: Time to Thrive (2015)

Alisa Smith grew up in Nigeria, West Africa as the child of missionary doctors. She is a graduate of Duke University who became a freelance writer after a career as an intensive care nurse. She lives in Chapel Hill, NC with her husband, animals, children and grandchildren nearby.
Chicken Soup for the Soul: Thanks to My Mom (2015)

Diane Stark is a former teacher turned stay-at-home mom and freelance writer. She loves to write about the important things in life: her family and her faith. She is the author of *Teachers' Devotions to Go*. E-mail her at DianeStark19@yahoo.com.
Chicken Soup for the Soul: Inspiration for Writers (2013)

Noelle Sterne publishes essays, writes craft articles, and spiritual pieces in many venues. With a Ph.D. (Columbia University), Noelle coaches doctoral candidates to dissertation completion. Her book, *Trust Your Life: Forgive Yourself and Go After Your Dreams* (Unity Books), helps readers release regrets, re-label their pasts, and reach lifelong yearnings.
Chicken Soup for the Soul: Just Us Girls (2013)

Natasha Stoynoff is a New York Times bestselling author. She has been a news reporter/photographer for the *Toronto Star*, *Time* magazine, and columnist/feature writer for the *Toronto Sun*. She's covered celebrities for *People* magazine for nearly two decades. Natasha lives in Manhattan and is working on her second screenplay.
Chicken Soup for the Soul: Hope & Miracles (2015)

Alexis Streb was born in 1997 and has always been a Navy brat. She has been all over the world, from Guam, to D.C. and back again. Alexis is a homeschooled vegetarian who reads and plays soccer all the time. E-mail her at alexis.streb@hotmail.com.
Chicken Soup for the Soul: Just for Teenagers (2011)

JC Sullivan is a member of the Travelers Century Club (www.travelerscenturyclub.org). Having worked in virtually every industry, she took her own advice and escaped the cubicle! Now she visits one new place a month and tries to do one thing a day that scares her. E-mail her at JobfreeJennifer@yahoo.com.
Chicken Soup for the Soul: Find Your Happiness (2011)

Susan Tornga lives and writes in southern Arizona. She enjoys hiking in the beautiful Sonoran Desert and traveling throughout this fascinating world of ours. She writes mysteries, both historical and current day, that celebrate the courage of women in the West. E-mail her at susantornga.writer@comcast.net.
Chicken Soup for the Soul: Inspiration for the Young at Heart (2011)

Cristy Trandahl is a former teacher and writer for the nation's leading student progress monitoring company. Today she works as a freelance writer while raising her children. Visit www.cristytrandahl.com for more.
Chicken Soup for the Soul: My Resolution (2008)

Marilyn Turk received her B.A. degree in journalism from LSU and has been published in *Guideposts*, *The Upper Room*, *Clubhouse Jr.*, *Coastal Christian Family*, and *Chicken Soup for the Soul*. She and husband Chuck enjoy fishing and playing tennis. She is writing a Christian historical novel. Learn more at Pathwayheart.com.
Chicken Soup for the Soul: Say Goodbye to Stress (2012)

Kristi Woods loves a sunny day and clicking words of encouragement onto the screen of www.KristiWoods.net. She, her retired-from-the-military husband, their three children, and several rescued pets survived the nomadic military lifestyle and have set roots in Oklahoma. Kristi writes Christian nonfiction.
Chicken Soup for the Soul: Dreams and Premonitions (2015)

ABOUT THE AUTHOR

 Amy Newmark is the bestselling author, editor-in-chief, and publisher of the *Chicken Soup for the Soul* book series. Since 2008, she has published 133 new books, most of them national bestsellers in the U.S. and Canada, more than doubling the number of *Chicken Soup for the Soul* titles in print today.

Amy is credited with revitalizing the Chicken Soup for the Soul brand, which has been a publishing industry phenomenon since the first book came out in 1993. By compiling inspirational and aspirational true stories curated from ordinary people who have had extraordinary experiences, Amy has kept the twenty-three-year-old Chicken Soup for the Soul brand fresh and relevant.

Amy graduated *magna cum laude* from Harvard University where she majored in Portuguese and minored in French. She then embarked on a three-decade career as a Wall Street analyst, a hedge fund manager, and a corporate executive in the technology field. She is a Chartered Financial Analyst, which will only mean something to you if you are on Wall Street!

Her return to literary pursuits was inevitable, as her honors thesis in college involved traveling throughout Brazil's impoverished northeast region, collecting stories from regular people. She is delighted to have come full circle in her writing career — from collecting stories "from the people" in Brazil as a twenty-year-old to, three decades later, collecting stories "from the people" for

Chicken Soup for the Soul.

When Amy and her husband Bill, the CEO of Chicken Soup for the Soul, are not working, they are visiting their four grown children.

Follow Amy on Twitter @amynewmark. Listen to her free daily podcast, The Chicken Soup for the Soul Podcast, at www.chickensoup.podbean.com, or find it on iTunes, the Podcasts app on iPhone, or on your favorite podcast app on other devices.

You can reach Amy at amy@chickensoupforthesoul.com.

Changing your life one story at a time®
www.chickensoup.com